The Illustrated Lives of the Great Composers

Sir Arthur

Bliss

John Sugden

OMNIBUS PRESS

LONDON · NEW YORK · SYDNEY

*This book is dedicated to
Lady Bliss, with gratitude.*

Copyright © 1997 Omnibus press
(A Division of Book Sales Limited)

Book edited byRoger and Elizabeth Buckley
Book typeset by Vitaset, Paddock Wood, Kent
Book Produced by Octave Books, Speldhurst, Kent
Cover Design and art direction by Studio Twenty, London
Cover photography by George Taylor

ISBN: 0.7119.6527.7
Order No: OP 47892

Exclusive Distributors:
Book Sales Limited,
8/9 Frith Street,
London W1V 5TZ, UK.

Music Sales Corporation,
257 Park Avenue South,
New York, NY 10010, USA.

Music Sales Pty Limited,
120 Rothschild Avenue,
Rosebury, NSW 2018, Australia.

To the Music Trade only:
Music Sales Limited,
8/9 Frith Street W1V 5TZ, UK.

Every effort has been made to trace the copyright holders of the photographs
in this book but one or two were unreachable. We would be grateful if the
photographers concerned would contact us.

Printed by Staples Printers Ltd, Rochester, Kent.

A catalogue record for this book is available from the British Library.

Visit Omnibus Press at http://www.musicsales.co.uk

Contents

Acknowledgements

All the illustrations, except when otherwise acknowledged, were provided by Lady Bliss, whose copyright they remain. The author and publishers are very grateful to her for permission to reproduce them and also for permission to quote from *As I Remember* (1989 edition).

The author also wishes to thank the following for their help in his research:

Mrs Elizabeth Travis, for invaluable assistance with photographs and documents.

Mr and Mrs R. Gatehouse
Mr and Mrs C. Sellick
Mr and Mrs G. Dannatt
Mr R. Andrewes (Head of Music, Cambridge University Library)
Mrs B. von Bethmann Holweg
Mr W. Blackshaw (Historian of Bilton Grange school)
Mr A. Burn (Bliss Trust)
Mr G. Easterbrook
Mrs N. Farquharson
Mr M. Freegard
Mr P. Horton (Librarian, Royal College of Music)
Mr D. Maclean (Archivist, Rugby School)
Miss J.S. Ringrose (Archivist, Pembroke College, Cambridge)
Mr L. Salter
Miss F. Southey (Novello & Co Ltd)
Mrs J. Waddell

1 School

I cannot remember any time when music was not part of my life. My mother was a fine pianist, and although she died when I was very young, the sound of music must have entered my ears from earliest days ... the playing of music was a natural instinct in the family.

Sir Arthur Bliss, 'Music', December 1951, pp.17–19

Arthur Edward Drummond Bliss was born on 2 August 1891 at his parents' house in Queen's Ride, Barnes, London. He was the eldest of three children, all boys; the second son, Francis Kennard, was born in September 1892, and the third, Howard James, in June 1894. In his autobiography *As I Remember*, first published in 1970, Arthur recalled the visits he and his brothers made to his grandmother's house by the river-side at Mortlake on occasional Sunday afternoons for tea. But by that time, sadly, his mother (formerly Agnes Kennard Davis) had died abroad and was buried in Mortlake Cemetery. The three young children hardly knew her but Arthur kept her photograph, which shows a handsome and elegant Victorian lady; he also kept her piano music which, he wrote later, was marked with her own phrasing and fingering and shows that '... she must have been a good amateur pianist.'[1]

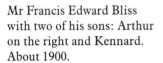

Mr Francis Edward Bliss with two of his sons: Arthur on the right and Kennard. About 1900.

After his mother died when he was three years old, Arthur and his two brothers moved with their father to a house in Holland Park, Kensington. The new house seemed 'very big and magnificent',[2] as Arthur wrote later, and his father staffed it with a housekeeper, a nanny and several servants. Mr Bliss was an American working in London with the Anglo-American Oil Company who belonged to the Old School; that is to say, a New Englander brought up on the strict principles of honour, duty and hard work which his forebears had inherited from the earliest settlers on the north-east coast. Looking at his portrait, one can fully empathize with his son's tribute in his autobiography:

I was supremely lucky not only in having such a father, to whom indeed I owe all that I may have myself achieved, but also in having one who by his own ability and hard work was able to give me the perfect environment in which to spend the years of my youth.[3]

1. Bliss *As I Remember*, Thames Publishing, 1989, p15.
2. Ibid. p16.
3. Ibid. pp16–17.

'Chamber Music': these two pictures show Arthur playing a piano solo and secondly, a trio with Kennard (left) on the clarinet and Howard playing the cello – both at their grandmother's house in Mortlake.

Number 21, Holland Park, Kensington: a sketch by Bridget Duckenfield of the house which became the Bliss family home after the death of Arthur's mother. (Reproduced with permission)

One would expect him to have been in tune with the late Victorian custom in which children should be seen and not heard, but he wasn't, at least so far as music was concerned. Mr Bliss encouraged his eldest boy to play his mother's piano and his other two sons to play respectively the clarinet and cello, so it was not very long before the elegant drawing room of No21 resounded to the tuneful Victorian music of a trio by Bache, perhaps, or by Jensen or Bohm, or even by one of those modern fellows like Eli Hudson. Whoever the composer, it must have been a sound which warmed a lonely widower's heart.

The three boys attended a local pre-preparatory school and also received dancing lessons at a nearby teacher's house where it seems that Arthur, at least, found the etiquette a little too formal for his liking. Maybe he was now ready, at the age of eight, to be plucked from these genteel surroundings and packed off to a boarding school – one not too near home but not too distant for a parent to visit in an emergency. The one chosen by his father was Bilton Grange, a large converted country house in its own grounds near the village of Dunchurch, about three miles south of Rugby. There, the Rev. Ernest Earle presided as Headmaster over about a hundred and twenty boys between the ages of eight and thirteen. At the latter age they would take an entrance examination for the secondary school of their parents' choice; about one third of them generally chose Rugby, as Mr Bliss did. But for Arthur that hurdle was five years ahead and meanwhile he had to cope with the ups and downs of boarding school life on his own initiative, for it was over a year before he was joined there by his middle brother, Kennard.

The first time Arthur Bliss's name appears in the school records is in the midsummer term's prize list for 1902 when he shared the prize for classics in Class V and won the prize for French outright. The presentation-book, bound in red leather with gold tooling, is inscribed on the front fly-leaf:

> Arthur E. Bliss
> Bilton. July 1902
> French Class 5
> Ernest H. Earle

Its title is *Star Land* by Sir Robert Stawell Ball FRS – 'being talks with young people about the wonders of the heavens' (Cassell & Co Ltd 1899). It is now part of the Bliss archive at the University Library, Cambridge. Its condition is pristine and there are no obvious signs of usage.

This promising academic start was maintained and two years later Arthur won the mathematics prize for his class, while his father did his best to widen the interests of any boys who found their way into the school library by presenting three books about bird-life in America. However, Arthur's main interest was quickly established in the field of music, his name and those of his two

The family car – probably a Renault of about 1905 – with Mr Bliss, Arthur and Miss Whitefoord (known to the boys as 'Duddle') in the back seat and the other two boys facing them. The head chauffeur, at the wheel, had previously been the coachman.

brothers appearing in practically every music programme recorded in the school magazine at that time.

For a school of its size, Bilton Grange was remarkably successful in promoting music; in 1903, for example, 89 boys were learning some instrument, while 70 were learning singing; almost every Sunday evening there was an informal concert, as the Magazine reported: 'We are glad to say that the Sunday evening music in the Lecture Hall, which at one time was almost entirely rendered by the masters, is now to a great extent given by the boys.'[1] On occasional week-ends there were talks or performances by visitors, some of them distinguished musicians. By a remarkable coincidence, Arthur came face-to-face on two such occasions with men who were to make a profound impression on his later career: first, E.J. Dent from Cambridge, himself an Old Biltonian. From the *Bilton Record*: 'On Saturday, November 21st, we were favoured with a visit from E.J. Dent, Esq., M.A. Mus. Bac. Fellow of King's College, Cambridge … The string Band played two pieces, there were two piano duets, a piano solo and a violin solo, whilst all three choirs sang in turn. Further music was rendered on the Sunday evening following, Mr. Dent also giving us two pianoforte solos. At the close, Mr. Dent expressed himself as highly pleased at what he had heard, commenting on each item of the previous evening. His remarks, if flattering, were certainly

1. *The Bilton Record*, July 1903, p73.

Bilton Grange: part of the main building.
(Courtesy of Bilton Grange School)

very encouraging, and should stimulate vocalists and instrumentalists alike to further and higher efforts.'[1] Dent was later 'the most stimulating influence'[2] whom Bliss encountered at university.

The other well known musician who visited the school while Arthur was a boy there – later to be his piano professor at the RCM – was Herbert Fryer, a friend of Mr Lucas, the Music Director of the school. As Cyril Smith, another of Fryer's pupils wrote: 'I doubt if England will ever produce another Herbert Fryer. What a list of pupils ... Arthur Bliss, Constant Lambert, Kendall Taylor, Lance Dossor, Colin Horsley ... were all taught by him.'[3] The *Bilton Record* was equally enthusiastic: 'His brilliancy of execution fairly roused the enthusiasm of his audience and he most kindly responded to all the encores ... We owe to Mr Lucas a debt of thanks for having induced his friend to come amongst us, and hope that this visit will not be the last.'[4] It was only the beginning for Arthur Bliss, but surely a very stimulating one.

In September 1904, the start of Arthur's last year at the School, his youngest brother, Howard, arrived as a new boy (known as Bliss min. while his two elder brothers were there) and had the doubtful pleasure of experiencing the discipline of Arthur who had just been made a Prefect. Perhaps Bliss min. found some compensation in watching his two elder siblings dressed up in silk stockings and pantaloons for their parts in a comedy by

1. *The Bilton Record*, July 1903, p73.
2. Bliss, op. cit. p27.
3. Smith, Cyril, *Duet for Three Hands*, Angus Robertson, 1958, p30.
4. Op. cit. July 1903, p90.

PROGRAMME.

1. Choral Ballad ... ... "The Miller's Wooing" ... ... *Eaton Faning.*
2. Songs ... ... "Two Lyrics" ... ... *Lane Wilson.*
   Mr. R. Crawshaw.
3. Violin Solo... ... ... "Sarabande" ... ... *Bohm.*
   Mr. A. W. Ogilvy.
4. Vocal Quartet ... "A wet sheet and a flowing sea" ... *C. H. Lloyd.*
   Mr. W. W. Cheriton, Mr. A. G. Youngman, Mr. H. Lyon, Mr. P. T. Lucas.
5. Pianoforte Duets :—(a) "Anitra's Dance" ⎫
   (b) "In the Hall of the Mountain King" ⎬ ... *Grieg.*
   A. E. D. Bliss, P. V. Anstruther. ⎭
6. A Scotch Rhapsody for Treble Voices ... ... *C. Vincent.*
7. Recit. and Song from "Iolanthe" ... ... *Sullivan.*
   Mr. H. Lyon.
8. Part Song for Men's Voices "The Beleaguered" ... ... *Sullivan.*
9. Violoncello Solo ... ... ⎰ "Canzonetta" ... ... *W. H. Squire.*
   ⎱ "Gavotte," Op. 23. ... ... *Popper.*
   J. H. Bliss.
10. Song ... ... "Border Ballad" ... ... *Cowen.*
    Mr. R. Crawshaw.
11. Vocal Quartet ... .. "The Goslings" ... ... *J. F. Bridge.*
    Mr. W. W. Cheriton, Mr. A. G. Youngman, Mr. H. Lyon, Mr. P. T. Lucas.
12. Pianoforte Solos :—(a) "Polonaise," Op. 40, No. 1. ... ... *Chopin.*
    (b) "Etude," in E minor ... ... *Poldini.*
    Mr. P. T. Lucas.
13. Part Songs... ... "Boat Song" ... ... *Cowen.*
    "O, my luve's like a red, red rose" ... ... *Garrett.*
14. Songs ... ... (a) "The little Irish Girl" ... ... *Löhr.*
    (b) "The little Red Fox" ... ... *Somervell.*

Two brothers in the same concert (see items 5 and 9). Success for Bliss min. but a slight lapse for *The Harmonious Blacksmith* in March, 1905. (Courtesy of Bilton Grange School)

---

4. Pianoforte Solo -	- "Study" -	- -	- *Heller*
	C. H. B. HERTZBERG.		
5. Violincello Solos -	- ⎰ a. "Chanson de Matin" -	-	*Edward Elgar*
	⎱ b. "Danse Orientale" -	-	- *W. H. Squire*
	J. H. BLISS.		
6. Songs - -	- ⎰ a. "Where the bee sucks" -	-	- *Arne*
	⎱ b. "Bright and joyous" -	-	- *C. Vincent*
	THE SECOND CHOIR.		
7. Pianoforte Duet -	- - "Idylle Arabe" -	-	- *Chaminade*
	R. A. BODDINGTON, E. H. S. EVANS.		
8. Strings and Pianoforte -	⎰ a. "Barcarolle" -	-	- *A. W. Ogilvy*
	⎱ b. "Valse Bohémienne" -	-	*S. Coleridge-Taylor*
9. Pianoforte Solo -	- "The Harmonious Blacksmith" -	-	*Handel*
	A. E. D. BLISS.		
10. Part Songs -	- ⎰ a. "Love and Summer" -	-	- *J. E. West*
	⎱ b. "Song of the Vikings" -	-	- *Eaton Faning*
	THE FIRST CHOIR.		
	GOD SAVE THE KING.		

Molière, drama being another activity encouraged by the school. In fact, during that year all three brothers featured many times in programmes of music, including that concert amusingly described in his autobiography when Arthur discovered, while on the platform, that he was definitely not cut out to be a concert-pianist: 'As I dilly-dallied with my piano-stool, my mind went blank, and the simple statement on which the Variations are based completely eluded me. After an anguished moment of indecision I plunged recklessly into a later variation ...'[1] This mortifying experience was delicately glossed over by the report in the magazine: '... Bliss ma's rendering of the *Harmonious Blacksmith* from memory was an evidence of much careful practice.'[2] But the lesson was well learnt and Bliss had the last word on this incident: 'Recollections of early failures cast long shadows, and to-day, even when conducting my own music ... I keep a score before me in case a similar lapse of memory should harrass me.'[3]

Bilton Grange also excelled in sports (cricket, hockey, rugby football and gymnastics) but there is no record of Bliss's achievements in any of these and the conclusion must be that he was, as a young boy, one of the long-suffering majority who stood near the boundary and lent an air of expectancy to the game. But by the time he had been at Rugby for a few years the picture was quite different; he was in his House XV, ran for his House (W.N. Wilson's) and fenced for the school, winning a medal for foil-fencing at the Public Schools Competition at Aldershot in 1910, his last year. He also played in the House Cricket final but, sad to say, did not trouble the scorers in either innings. All the same, in the Order of Houses at the end of the year Wilson's came second and Bliss's contribution to its success was not negligible.

Each house at most public schools at that time was a separate entity and the boys were expected to give their primary loyalty to it, unless they were representing the school. The houses at Rugby, except for School House, were dispersed around the town; parents would often specify which house they preferred for their son when applying for entrance. The Housemaster and his wife (or House-keeper if he was a bachelor) ran the house literally as a boarding-house, taking a share of the profit from fees, such as it was, at the end of the school year. This system (now abandoned in most boarding schools in favour of a more centralized administration) meant that all the aspects of life which, in retrospect, would appear trivial but at the time assumed enormous importance, stemmed from the rules and regulations laid down by the Housemaster. How you dressed, which jacket-buttons could be left undone, into which pockets you could put your hands, at what angle you wore your straw boater, on which side of the street you walked – all these trivialities and many more were decided and decreed by your House and enforced by the Praeposters, guardians of house and school discipline. So in many respects the house *was* the school, in the same sense that the school *was* the town.

1. Bliss, op.cit. p19   2. Op.cit . August 1905   3. Bliss, op.cit. p20

Not surprisingly, young Bliss found that life at Rugby was all-absorbing: 'What great events were taking place in the world during the years 1905-10 while I was at Rugby? Who was in power, who was dethroned? Who had conquered, who had lost? Without looking at a history of the period, I could not now give any account of those global matters. The small but infinitely dramatic and hazardous doings in the microcosm of Rugby absorbed me entirely ...'[1] he wrote sixty years later. To be fair, they were probably ignored by most of the young people at Rugby and at other boarding schools in Britain.

But Bliss had another overriding reason for cutting himself off from the outside world, one which made him impervious to many troubles and changes going on around him and which stayed with him all his life – his music. It was at Rugby that he first heard a public performance of one of his own compositions, in the house of the school's Director of Music, Basil Johnson. This was a chastening experience which he describes with disarming modesty in his autobiography.[2] There were other musical occasions of a more formal kind taking place at the school then which demanded his attention: he must certainly have taken part in the chorus at the end of the first concert given in the new Speech Room on the evening of its official opening by King Edward VII (3 July 1909). There is a brief mention of this event

3 July 1909 – King Edward VII arriving at Rugby School to open the new Speech Room. The Headmaster, Dr H.A. James – nicknamed 'The Bodger' – is in the foreground.
(Courtesy of Rugby School)

1. Bliss, op. cit. p21.   2. Bliss, op. cit. p20.

in the autobiography[1] but his memory failed him when he wrote that he did not see the Speech Room again until he returned to conduct his Cantata, *The Beatitudes*, in 1962. In fact, he performed at three concerts in the Speech Room during his last year at Rugby, first on 18 December 1909, when *The Meteor* (the school magazine) reported that he 'acquitted himself very brilliantly'[2] in a duet, *Theme and Variations*, for two pianos by Arensky; second, when he sang in the chorus for a performance of *The Dream of Gerontius* (see below); and third, at the end of his last term when he played two piano solos[3] (see illustrations).

Bliss acknowledges a growing love for the music of Elgar during his time at Rugby and says that taking part in *Gerontius* 'put the seal on [his] fervent admiration'.[4] This performance was described in *The Meteor* in some detail; evidently the audience was given a talk about the work before it started to help their understanding of it: 'A most interesting lecture was given ... on the words and music by Mr David and Mr Johnson, which must have done a great deal to make the actual performance more enjoyable to many members of the School, since the music at least, to one who hears it for the first time, must seem absolutely unintelligible.'[5]

Bliss's love for Elgar's music never left him. He appreciated that an intimately known area of countryside could often have a profound effect on composition and, in Elgar's case, he concluded that this provides a key to comprehending his music. But in later life he derided the popular bowler-hat-and-shooting-stick image of him which, he surmises, may have been merely 'a decoy to lure the inquisitive away from private preserves.'[6] This insight into a composer's private world is one of the few revealed by Bliss in his writings and is very significant since he himself developed an image in old age, not entirely dissimilar from Elgar's, of the benevolent retired-country-gentleman-in-tweeds. It is impossible not to wonder how much this image had the same purpose as that which he ascribed to Elgar.

A completely different image which Bliss recalled from his Rugby days is that of the eccentric, wound-up classics master, 'quivering with excitement'[7] as he read aloud purple passages from Homer or Shakespeare and thus inspired the seventeen-year-old with a lasting affection and regard for the ancient languages and exemplary texts; and at this impressionable age there must also have been a touch of awe and wonder on the part of a sensitive and highly intelligent young man. The classical myths and ancient legends held him in thrall for life.

The master responsible for this lasting influence on Bliss was Robert Whitelaw, godfather of Rupert Brooke, 'an inspired teacher',[8] according to Bliss, but according to his godson the same

1. Bliss, op. cit. p20.
2. *The Meteor*, 16 Feb. 1910, p6.
3. Ibid. 25 July 1910.
4. Bliss, op.cit. p23.
5. *The Meteor*, 5 April 1910, p35.
6. Bliss, op.cit. p25.
7. Ibid.
8. Ibid.

Rugby School Concert.

MONDAY, JULY 25th, 1910,

AT EIGHT O'CLOCK,

IN THE

SPEECH ROOM.

man was an example of the worst sort of sarcastic pedagogue,[1] which shows how widely some pupils can differ in their response to the same teacher.

To summarise Arthur Bliss's schooling and the extent to which he responded to its various influences, I think it would be true to say that in his autobiography he did neither school full justice. This may have been partly due to not keeping a diary or any written reminiscence of those years, and partly to lack of space, but recognition of the opportunities both schools gave him to develop his musical talent is lacking in the autobiography and the complaint that, 'In my time [at Rugby] any boy who showed a determination to become a musician was *rara avis*, to be treated

1. See Christopher Hassall, *Rupert Brooke*, Faber Paperbacks 1984, pp39-40.

PROGRAMME.

PART I.

1. OVERTURE ..."Le Nozze di Figaro" ... ... *Mozart*

2. "THE REVENGE," FOR CHORUS AND ORCHESTRA *Stanford*

3. ORGAN ... From the "Suite Gothique "... *Boellmann*
   Andante. *Allegro.*
   B. W. FAGAN.

PART II.

1. OCTET FOR STRINGS (First movement) ... *Mendelssohn*

Mr. YUILLE-SMITH.	Mr. A. H. CASTLE.
K. H. M. SUTTON.	Miss MASSIAH.
C. H. GLOVER.	Mrs. COLE.
Mrs. BRADBY and }	Mr. A. E. DONKIN.
T. H. MARSHALL }	

2. PART SONG ... "The Fairies" ... *Stanford*

3. PIANOFORTE ... *(a)* "Rêve étrange" ... *Moskowski*
   (b) "Romance"... ... ...*Sibelius*
   A. E. BLISS.

4. SONGS ... *(a)* "Life's Epitome " ... *Kenneth Rae*
   (b) "Chanson de Florian " ...*Godard*
   C. R. COOTE.

5. VIOLONCELLO SOLO "Romance in F " ... ...*Fischer*
   C. F. B. SIMPSON.

6. PART SONG "Purple glow the forest mountains " *Pearsal*

7. SLAVISCHE TANZ FOR ORCHESTRA ... ...*Dvorak*

8. CARMEN FERIALE "Floreat Rugbeia" *Rev. C. E. Moberly*

GOD SAVE THE KING.

PART I.

1. OVERTURE ..."Le Nozze di Figaro " ... ...*Mozart*

2. "THE REVENGE," FOR CHORUS AND ORCHESTRA *Stanford*

A Ballad of the Fleet.

Words by Lord Tennyson.

The singular sea-fight, in which Sir Richard Grenville's vessel, *The Revenge*, figured, is described as follows by Miss Yonge in her "Cameos from English History." " At the Azores Lord Thomas Howard and Sir Richard Grenville watched in 1591 for the carracks," *i.e.* Spanish treasure ships coming home loaded from the mines of Mexico and Peru), "but instead of meeting them were attacked by the fleet under Don Alfonso de Bassano, whom Philip II. sent out on discovering their purpose. The English were carelessly waiting the carracks, when from behind the island the huge fleet of fifty-three men-of-war appeared so near them that they had hardly time to weigh anchor. Many of the men were sick, many on shore, all was confusion, but Howard contrived to get away with all the ships save that of Grenville, who wanted to get the men ashore on board, refusing to forsake them and thus to 'dishonour himself, his country and Her Majesty's ships.' He then proceeded with his one vessel, the *Revenge*, to fight his way through the whole of the enemy's fleet. Five vessels attacked him at once. Again and again he beat off his assailants, sorely damaged, and for fifteen hours kept up the fight till his masts being shattered, his tackle gone, his powder spent, forty men killed, and himself desperately wounded, he bade the master gunner sink the ship, lest it should fall into the enemy's hands. The survivors, however, took the matter into their own hands, and surrendered. Don Alfonso wished to remove Sir Richard from the *Revenge*, which was like a slaughter-house, but he refused to leave it with his own consent. However, with all honour he was taken on board a Spanish ship, where he died two days after, saying, 'Here die I, Richard Grenville, with a joyful and quiet mind, having ended my life as a good soldier ought to do.' "

with a good deal of condescension, if not worse ..."[1] is to beg the question: what worse treatment? No satisfactory answer is provided, unfortunately.

However, we must not forget that in those days, when holidays were a little longer than they are now, they accounted for about one third of the year and Bliss describes their joys in glowing terms. His father naturally indulged all his three boys during their holidays but one imagines that he missed no opportunity for furthering their education at the same time, either in London or in the country, so it may well be that Arthur owed his cultivation and erudition at the age of eighteen as much to his parent as to his schooling. We may imagine him as he left Rugby at the end of the summer in 1910, a gangling young man, with a shock of brown hair and a rather pre-occupied, far-away look in his eyes, confident and self-possessed but receptive to ideas, especially artistic ones, and enthusiastic about everything new. The ideal candidate, it would seem, for higher education and university life.

1. Bliss, op. cit. p20.

2 University and First War

Call not thy wanderer home as yet
Though it be late.
Now is his first assailing of
The invisible gate.
Be still through that light knocking. The hour
Is throng'd with fate.

George William Russell, 'Germinal'

The University of Cambridge in 1910 was a place of sheer delight, mixed with a few dangers. The delights were obvious – two colleges for young ladies (Girton and Newnham)[1], many societies covering almost every imaginable intellectual interest, and unlimited opportunites for sport – either as a serious occupation or merely for exercise and enjoyment with like-minded friends. The dangers, by comparison, were minimal but more insidious: primarily, the temptation to allow pleasure to supplant work as a priority, but also the danger of allowing frivolity to overtake sincerity as an attitude of mind.

Arthur Bliss was naturally susceptible to all these elements. He liked people, of both sexes, he was companionable and friendly and his activities were not too severely restricted by financial restraints. The three years which he spent at the University, between the ages of nineteen and twenty-two, must have flown by like a video-tape in the 'fast forward' setting because he retained only kaleidoscopic visions of them in the memory:

What I discern in these 'flash-backs' is, with the days, the weeks, the months imperceptibly slipping by, a sporadic and undirected excitement, and a reluctance to concentrate, except haphazardly, on the central core of my being, my music. Life with a very large capital L was too delicious just to breathe in, and I think that I mortgaged the immediate future by this dilettantism, just when I should have closed the doors on a good slice of life and locked myself in with my work.[2]

He devoted only two pages of his autobiography to these years and left no diaries or notes about his friends at Pembroke College, his rooms there, his attitude to wider topics like religion, literature, drama, or his hopes and ambitions related to his eventual degree. We do know that on his application for admission, he stated that he intended to read for the Classical Tripos but in fact

1. Female students at Cambridge were not allowed to take degrees until after 1918, and were not granted full degrees until 1947.
2. Bliss, op. cit. p28.

he read for an ordinary degree in history, gaining second class honours in Part I (in 1911) and a first class in Part II (1913). Concurrently, he read for the degree of Bachelor of Music achieving the high honour of a First in Part I and completing the course two years later, but no record exists for the result in this second part. One interpretation of this could be that he came near to achieving a Double First in history and music but that for some reason (health or stress?) he failed to clear the last hurdle in music. While some lapse of attainment seems entirely forgivable, at the end of such a crowded course of study, whether that is what actually happened, or whether the records are simply incomplete, we may never know.

There are few compositions by Bliss at Cambridge in the catalogue of his works, although he says in the autobiography that he and some friends formed a society 'which regularly met to read and play each other's works in a mood of mutual admiration.'[1] They also indulged in the customary 'extravaganza', as Bliss calls it, of dressing up and hiring a bus to drive them round Cambridge while they made merry with a feast no doubt imported from college kitchens. He mentions long summer afternoons in a punt on the river and long evenings spent in discussion about 'everything and nothing' but without full details it is impossible to gain a clear picture of his life as an undergraduate, and perhaps that was his intention.

One positive identification is the influence of Edward Dent and, through him, of his friend and teacher Busoni. Dent had recently returned to Cambridge after a long sabbatical in Europe and was able to pass on to his students the latest Continental ideas about the interpretation of the nineteenth-century romantics. This was important in a wider musical context, for there was then a strong surge of reaction among young intellectuals against what they identified as the 'sentimental' element in romanticism. They associated this with the Victorian age and consequently included it in their criticism of all the conventions of that period which they found restricting and dated. One amusing inconsistency of this reaction was that the same young academics who supported it so vociferously were, in many cases, intensely sentimental in their own relationships.[2]

Bliss could not possibly have failed to be caught up in this flow of opinion about the century which had recently ended. He must have been looking round with keen interest at the contemporary influences on British composers and, however much he was still enthralled by Elgar's music or more recently intoxicated with that of Vaughan Williams,[3] his early flirtations with Ravel and Debussy had already signified a willingness to seek inspiration further afield when needed.[4] This is where Dent's impact at

1. Ibid. p27.
2. See the excellent biography by Christopher Hassall of Rupert Brooke (Faber Paperbacks 1972 reprinted 1984).
3. Bliss op. cit. p26.   4. Ibid p21.

TO MY FATHER.

Suite for Piano

Prelude – Ballade – Scherzo

ARTHUR BLISS

Copyright.

Price 1/6 net.

LONDON:

JOSEPH WILLIAMS, Limited,
32, Great Portland Street, W.

Left: The front cover of 'Suite for Piano', dedicated to his father, which Bliss composed while up at Cambridge.

Right: 'I am very bankrupt now …' is the perpetual cry of the student but this one had something to sell. His letter is to a friend who had gone down the previous year and who was, presumably, employed by the publisher Joseph Williams.

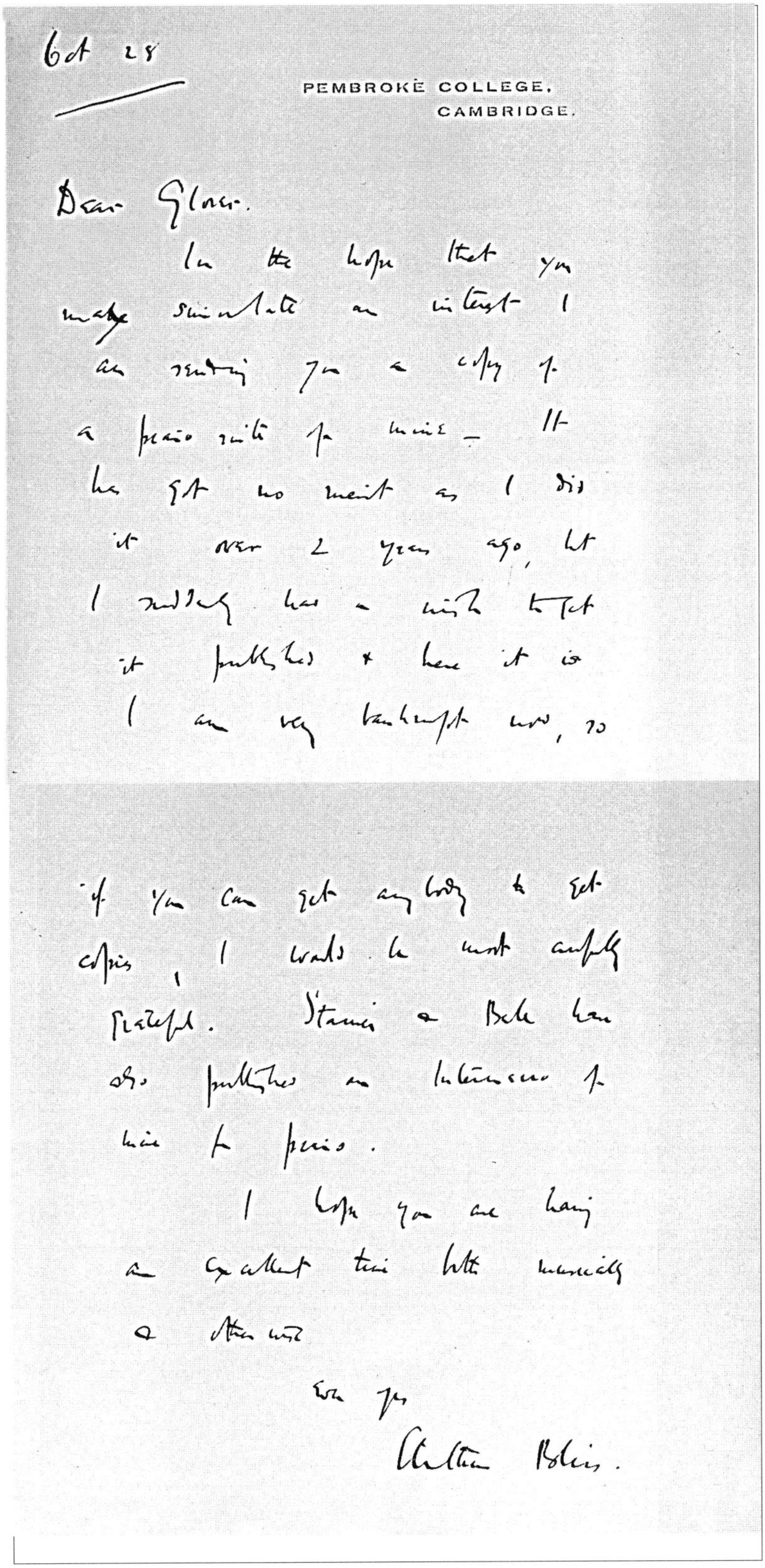

Oct 28

PEMBROKE COLLEGE,
CAMBRIDGE.

Dear Glover.

In the hope that you may stimulate an interest I am sending you a copy of a piano suite of mine — It has got no merit as I did it over 2 years ago, but I suddenly had a wish to get it published & here it is. I am very bankrupt now, so if you can get anybody to get copies, I would be most awfully grateful. Stainer & Bell have also published an Intermezzo of mine for piano.

I hope you are having an excellent time both musically & otherwise.

Ever yrs

Arthur Bliss.

Cambridge was significant; it provided a direct and immediate contact with the current European designs in music and gave Bliss some valuable pointers for the future.

This is about as far as we can see into the university career of Arthur Bliss. His later musical achievements, together with his writings, show him to have been academically minded, well read and capable of deep thought; he also possessed a most attractive and clear style of writing, as his autobiography shows. But none of these considerable assets appear to have been fully recognized while he was an undergraduate and it was much later when the University – and his College – awarded him the honours due to him. In February 1964, he and Michael Tippett were given honorary Doctorates of Music at a ceremony in the Senate House, when the University Orator reminded the audience that music degrees at Cambridge had first been conferred 500 years previously. In fact, this Quincentenary had been celebrated two days earlier by the first performance of Bliss's *Golden Cantata*, a commissioned work for solo tenor, chorus and orchestra, with words by Kathleen Raine, conducted by the composer. It was fitting that, nearly fifty years late, as it were, Bliss should have been described by the Orator as 'a son of Cambridge'.[1] Both he and the University took a little time to recognize each other as *primus inter pares*.

In 1913, when Bliss left Cambridge, the so-called 'Bloomsbury Group' of artists, writers and intellectuals were in full cry, pouring their satirical scorn on all things British and especially on all those conventions which had spilled over from the Victorian age. The influence of the Woolfs, the Bells, Roger Fry, Lytton Strachey and J. Maynard Keynes was considerable among all the young intellectuals of the period. Although, as they grew older and wiser, they began to apply positive remedies to the ills which they had discovered in the culture of the previous generation, this group left a strong negative attitude among their admirers and disciples. There was a surge of discontent with authority in the student population.

There is no evidence to suggest that Arthur Bliss was associated in any way with the Bloomsbury set but it would have been impossible for him at Cambridge, and later in London, not to have been aware of the 'spirit of the age' and of the revolt against conventional attitudes going on all around him. He wrote, 'at twenty-two I was too old to conform ... I regarded the defiant attitude ... as the only right one for a student.'[2]

There is just a glimpse of this defiance in his comments on the minor contact he had with Charles Stanford, Professor of Compositon at the Royal College of Music, where Bliss was a student after coming down from Cambridge: 'I felt the lack of sympathy betwen us ... he had a devitalizing effect on me.'[3] With

'A son of Cambridge ...': Sir Arthur Bliss and Michael Tippett were awarded Honorary Doctorates of Music by the University in 1964.
(Courtesy of *Cambridge Evening News*)

1. *Cambridge News* 20 February 1964, p14.
2. Bliss, op. cit. p29.
3. Ibid.

Hubert Parry, the Director, he had much more sympathy but even less contact. The main influence during this year at the Royal College of Music was Stravinsky and that influence was, of course, indirect. Bliss describes briefly how he and his friends – Herbert Howells, Eugene Goossens and Arthur Benjamin – went to the Diaghilev ballet productions at Drury Lane and how these evenings were 'shot through with unexpected excitements, as the curtain went up on a Bakst design or the opening notes of a Stravinsky score were heard.'[1]

Of these Stravinsky ballets, it was *Petrushka* which seems to have made the deepest and most universal impression. In fact, not only Bliss, Howells and Goossens but also Vaughan Williams, Holst, Walton, Bax, Ireland and Lambert have all been said to belong to 'the *Petrushka* generation in England'[2] indicating that Bliss was already in affinity with a type of music different – especially in orchestration – from the more ponderous tones of Brahms and Elgar. Shortly after the War, which was now threatening, Bliss wrote; 'in Petrouchka Stravinsky takes a step forward .... treating his various instruments as individuals, whose particular timbres should be investigated to the full, not solely as members of a family who worked in collusion for harmonic effect.'[3] In the light of Bliss's early published compositions, this is a significant judgement.

Howells was considered by his friends to possess 'the outstanding talent'[4] among his contemporaries and it was he who produced an orchestral suite first performed at the Royal College of Music in 1915 consisting of five movements all named after friends whose names, or nicknames, began with the letter B; hence the name of the suite, *The B's*. The first movment was called 'Bublum' (Howells himself) and the third (a scherzo) called 'Blissy'. Four years later, the suite was played again at Bournemouth by Sir Dan Godfrey in what Howells described as 'a magnificent performance'.[5] He revived two movements in 1948 as his contribution to a new work, *Music for a Prince* (i.e. the Prince of Wales), to which Tippett and Jacob also contributed; one of Howell's movements was 'Blissy', now re-named 'Scherzo in Arden'. Bliss's friendship with Howells continued until the death of the former (Howells died in 1983) but it couldn't be described as an intimate one because 'they were too fundamentally different in outlook and temperament for that.'[6]

A small taste of these differences in outlook may be had from a comparison of two letters, one written to Howells by Bliss near the end of the war in August 1918, the other by Howells to Bliss in October 1962. Both refer to anniversaries.

1. Ibid p28.
2. Christopher Palmer, *Herbert Howells, A Centenary Celebration*, Thames 1992, p181.
3. Bliss 'A Short Note on Stravinsky's Orchestration' quoted in *Bliss on Music* ed Gregory Roscow, OUP 1991 pp25-26.
4. Bliss op. cit. p28.
5. Palmer, op.cit. p374.
6. Ibid p26.

1. ... It is dreadful Herbert, to approach 30 with all one's ambitions held back from fruition by fate. How I hoped to be a modern da Vinci stamped with the characteristics of an Englishman – instead a humble subaltern of the Brigade of Guards with a leaning to musical expression, which no-one thinks much of, least of all the author ...[1]

2. You need no telling – surely? – how comforted and moved I am that a friendship of so long a time – yours and mine – should bring us together on our seventieth birthdays. For my part I cannot yet grasp how heartening it is to have so much affection flowing in upon one on these occasions.[2]

Of course the circumstances were quite different at the times when these letters were written but one can detect in the first an acceptance, even if born of frustration, of his destiny, always present when Bliss ruminated on the future, and in the second, a pleasurable, if surprised, realization that his destiny could be accompanied by the love of friends.

Bliss must certainly have composed music during the year before the outbreak of war, when he was at the College, but none of it was published in its original form. He explains in the autobiography[3] that he 'worked' in a room above a shop in Kensington but distraction from work, to which he was always prone, was not in the shape of the traffic outside the window but in that of a good-looking girl who exercised her dog each morning in the adjacent gardens and whom he managed to intercept 'by chance' occasionally.

Such innocent youthful amusement, however, was short-lived; the early summer of 1914 was the last period of peace he was to experience for the next four years. When the declaration of war came with a rush in August, he waited only a week before signing up at a recruiting office and a short time later found himself posted as a second lieutenant to a volunteer battalion of the 13th Royal Fusiliers. Thus it was that a twenty-three-year-old officer, 'unacquainted with matters military'[4] as he claimed (forgetting perhaps, that he had spent two years in the OTC at Rugby), was put in charge of a platoon of raw youngsters, who had similarly volunteered, and began training to face the mighty German army on the battlefields of France and Belgium. How often this scenario was repeated, with amateurish confidence, all over Britain.

Bliss explains[5] that the account of his war-experiences in extracts from a diary and from letters home is conditioned by his understandable wish to spare his father and relations too much detail of the dreadful events and conditions through which he lived. Consequently, the overall impression from his account is less horrifying, though no less interesting and moving, than many others. This raises an important point for a biographer of Arthur

1. Quoted by Palmer, op. cit. p28.
2. Op. cit. p29.
3. Bliss, op. cit. p29.
4. Ibid p30.
5. Ibid p32.

Bliss: why, throughout his own autobiography, was he so diffident about commenting on people – friends, personalities, other major contemporary figures? One answer (a valid one, I think) is that he was a very private person himself and so would not have wished to trespass on the privacy of others. Complementing this, he was very direct in all his relationships and would have deplored any temptation to embroider a personal judgement, or to exaggerate personal quirks in others in a theatrical way. At the same time, he was an excellent mimic – in private – according to his friends:

> ... Arthur Bliss was a born comic actor – he could 'take people off' so very well. For instance, in criticizing a rather poor play in which one of the characters was a bearded high member of the Church, he suddenly took out his white handkerchief, put it in his mouth so that it fell down well below his chin, and delivered the start of a pompous speech we had heard the evening before.

> Arthur loved to show off if he had a good audience and he decided ... to demonstrate the exercises which his physiotherapist made him do – so he lay flat on his back in front of the fire and proceeded to raise his legs in the air with many comic contortions, and a running commentary of hilarious fun ...

So why the diffidence when he was writing his memoirs? Perhaps the best explanation is contained in a letter he wrote to Eric Crozier,[1] the opera librettist and producer, who helped Bliss with the proofs of the book:

Arthur (*right*) and Kennard in uniform on the steps of 21 Holland Park in 1915.

> ... I think your criticism of 'the new feeling of shyness between myself and the reader' is a just one. The difficulty I find in 'As I Remember' when personalities ... are only met in transit, and in themselves leave me uninterested, (is) I cannot revitalise them. Perhaps I should leave all names out except those that are in some way alive to me to-day through some special memory ... This is a big subject and must be discussed over a good meal. May I implore your Argus eye again?[2]

The most remarkable fact about Bliss's war-experience from 1914 to 1918 was that he survived. About one in three British Army Officers were killed or seriously wounded on the Western Front, and in the infantry the proportion must have been at its greatest. From August to December 1915, Bliss's unit was in the front line trenches almost continuously and in the following July it was sent to the Somme sector to take part in the great battle of that name. It was during the attack on La Boisselle, which he described as a scene of confusion looking 'like Hampstead Heath on a Bank Holiday painted by a madman'[3] that he was wounded:

1. Crozier also collaborated with Arthur Bliss in 'Cradle Song for a Newborn Child' composed for the birth of HRH Prince Edward in 1963.
2. Letter from Arthur Bliss to Eric Crozier, 12 April 1967.
3. Bliss, op. cit. p40.

Somehow we stumbled into our trenches facing the Germans and waited. The enemy guns were so silent that either they had been silenced by our prolonged shelling or they were waiting. As we climbed out of the trench sharp at 8.30 am and advanced in a long extended line, we knew which alternative was the right one. They were waiting. I saw men falling on either flank and then I felt as though I had been struck a heavy blow on the leg by an iron bar. I fell in the mud and crawled to some hole for shelter. Later in the day ... stretcher bearers, those brave and welcome adjuncts to any attacking force, found me and took me down to the First Aid Post ...[1]

He described his wound (in the left leg) as a 'slight one' but it was sufficiently disabling for him to be sent back to England and to a hospital in London. While he was there, he received a satirical letter from his brother, Kennard, written on the last day of July:

Well, and I suppose you are looking forward to returning to the front, aren't you? Isn't the joy of sacrifice and the lust for honour hot within you again? [Arthur had recently been Mentioned in Despatches] Away with a life of ease and idle pleasure! Why waste money on an opera ticket, when you can present the Empire with a hand grenade?[3]

The family susequently received the news that Kennard had been killed (on 28 September) in the same battle of the Somme in which Arthur had been wounded.

Poet, painter, musician, he was the most gifted of us all and to me his rebellious nature would have been a stimulant, his caustic comments a sharp corrective through those years when I was struggling on my own for musical expression.[2]

It was more than a dozen years later that Arthur commemorated the loss of Kennard in music with the composition of *Morning Heroes*.

Arthur and Kennard were both sensitive artists (as Howard, the third brother, was also – but he was rejected for military service on medical grounds) and their reactions to the horror and beastliness of war were similar. Letters home always contained references to what they were reading – the poems of Shelley and Wordsworth, Tolstoy's *War and Peace*, the letters of Lamb to Coleridge, the essays of Bacon – and what gramophone records Arthur needed – 'Debussy's Quartet' (the slow movement), 'Overture and March' from *Prince Igor*, Tchaikovsky's 'Theme and Variations' in G. It was important, he explained, to have something worthwhile to listen to, to read, and to eat, in that order. He even asked for the libretto of Stanford's opera *The Critic*, while most of his comrades were requesting 'Daisy' or 'Tipperary' in their letters home. Every time he encountered an example of the

1. Ibid. pp40-41.
2. Ibid. p45.
3. Ibid. p42.

'Like Hampstead Heath … painted by a madman' was how Bliss described the scene on the Western Front in 1915. This picture shows how apt the description was.

live natural world among all the chaos, dirt and death, he stored it up in the memory as something to treasure. To such men, the conditions on the Western Front were a hideous nightmare to be expunged from the mind, whenever possible, by a few moments return to sanity with a book, or listening to music. Kennard regularly enquired about the latest recordings of Berlioz, his favourite, while Arthur actually managed (in 1915) to compose a string quartet and a piano quartet; these were sent home to his father who 'saw them through' Stainer and Novello and in the composer's absence they were performed in London but withdrawn after the War. While he was in England, Arthur had the time – and strangely enough the inclination – to steep himself in Wagner's 'Ring' while awaiting a new posting; however his own music contains no traces of the inhibitions such an influence sometimes induced.

A fleeting recollection of this period of sick-leave in 1917 was provided by Adrian Boult in his tribute to Sir Arthur Bliss on his 80th birthday ('Our most distinguished Ex-Collegian', as he describes him):

I first met him in 1917 when he was a Guard's Officer doing a special course near Bath, where I, strangely, was interviewing the local boot retailers on behalf of the War Office. A musical friend put me up for the night, and asked Arthur to dine with us. I shall never forget his delight and veneration when I showed him the manuscript of the Vaughan Williams London Sympohony, which had only then had two performances. We next met in the Courtyard of Buckingham Palace where he was in charge of a large group of the women who had done war jobs and were being inspected by King George V and Queen Mary. I was also on duty but as a Special Constable![1]

The Buckingham Palace incident is also described, rather more dramaticaly, by Bliss in his memoirs.[2] He follows it with an explanation of why he decided to transfer to the Grenadier Guards for what turned out to be his final period of active service, and how the prospect of a return to the Western Front affected him spiritually. His conviction during the first years of the war that he would survive, in spite of the odds against him, now began to waver:

As a family we had never held deep religious convictions: my father had a stern New England consciousness of what was right and what was wrong, and formal outward observance seemed superfluous. At School, at the age of Confirmation, it is true that I felt a momentary spiritual quickening but, with religious services relapsing into routine habit, whatever exaltation there had been soon faded palely away. But now I felt the urgent need for some reassurance that sudden death did not automatically annihilate the human soul: perhaps Faith could prove stronger than a stubborn disbelief. In search of a solution I went to a priest at the Brompton Oratory for instruction, and later was received into the Catholic church.[3]

There are scarcely any further references to his religious belief in the autobiography, or in his other published writings; indeed, any quotation regarding spiritual matters is confined to secular literature, often from Plato. And yet, in later life – certainly from 1956 onwards – he composed more than a dozen works on a religious theme; including his last big choral work *Shield of Faith* written in the last year of his life. At the end of her Chapter added as a 'coda' to her husband's memoirs, Lady Bliss quotes from a letter he wrote to a friend shortly before he died:

Belief should extend to the mystery beyond death. I am not convinced that this is the final shutting of the door.[4]

Perhaps he was originally converted to this persuasion by the priest at the Brompton Oratory who instructed him, and perhaps he was fortunate enough to carry it with him back to the trenches in France in September 1918. He would never have told anyone then; religious belief was to him a private matter and he kept it so, nearly to the end.

Bliss had been back in France for just over a month when he had the 'ill fortune' as he said, to swallow a gulp of poison gas during a night attack (the enemy was by then in retreat). He wrote home saying there was nothing to be anxious about but this

1. Adrian C. Boult, 'Sir Arthur Bliss', *Royal College of Music Magazine*, July 1982, p61.
2. Bliss, op. cit pp47-8.
3. Bliss, op. cit. pp48-9.
4. Bliss, op. cit. p228.

letter was from a base hospital in Rouen and his father must by now have dreaded seeing an address of this kind. To his brother Howard he was a little more explicit, confiding that he had collapsed after the inhalation of gas and had nearly been repatriated but not quite. He doesn't mention the Armistice of 11 November but describes his anger when he saw German NCO prisoners bullying their rank and file, which provoked him to intervene and put a stop to it.

Thus Bliss ended the war as he had begun it, outraged at injustice and persecution; otherwise content to go along with his destiny. In practical terms, he had survived because he was quick-witted and well organized, qualities which are abundantly clear from his carefully edited version of events. But as with all the other survivors, the memories haunted him for many years afterwards.

3 Recovery

Glory of youth glowed in his soul,
Where is that glory now?

R.L. Stevenson, 'Songs of Travel'

The year 1919 heard the première of Elgar's 'Cello Concerto', that elegy for departed souls and past times, and people wept not only for these but at the realization that the war had shattered belief in progress; what had *seemed* to be 'the improving years' of the new century now lay in ruins; idealism was a fiction, apparently. This possibility was too overwhelming for many to contemplate: the American writer Henry James (one of Arthur Bliss's favourite authors) said it was 'too tragic for any words', and he was not generally short of those. Others, usually referred to as 'the war poets', articulated different facets of the tragedy for at least two decades after the event, bringing their backward glances perilously close to the next twentieth century global disaster, which was just round the corner.

It was not surprising that the fresh-faced hopes of pre-war British music (epitomized by Elgar's *Wand of Youth* Suites) wore a different expression after the war had ended. Some composers – notably Vaughan Williams – returned to folk tunes for inspiration, finding there echoes of rural England to soothe the wounds of war. Elgar himself tried to revive his old enthusiasm but after the death of his wife in 1920 he wrote little of value comparable with the great pre-war symphonies and oratorios; towards the end of his own life he had to suffer the indignity of two small works (for male voice choir) being returned by the publisher because 'we cannot take them over from you on your terms.'[1] A far cry from twenty years before, when every music publisher in the country was competing for his works!

Other British composers from the pre-war period gradually found their feet again after 1918; for example: Delius at his country home in France, composing works which defy classification; Holst experiencing the popular success of his mystic suite *The Planets*; and the indomitable Ethel Smyth, created Dame shortly after the War and only ten years after serving a three-month jail sentence for militant suffragism. There was more than a touch of eccentricity in the musical climate of post-war Britain: of the younger composers, William Walton was catapulted into

---

1. Jerrold Northrop More, *Edward Elgar*, OUP 1987, p767.

Edward Elgar in 1916, the signed picture which he sent to Bliss while he was serving on the Western Front.

'Anyone for tennis?' – Adrian Boult, Ethel Smyth and Henry Wood look as if they need a fourth at Chorley Wood in 1926.

fame through his close association with the Sitwell family who were determined to pursue the avant-gardist tendency in literature and the arts, of which Walton's *Façade* – composed under the Sitwell aegis – was a leading example; it was first performed before a fashionable society audience in London in 1922. In that same year, the International Society for Contemporary Music (ISCM) was founded and presented its first series of concerts in Salzburg; one item on the programme (receiving its second public performance) was Arthur Bliss's chamber work, *Rout*.

The very name of the piece indicates the direction in which Bliss appeared to be going in 1920. He said (in *As I Remember*) that he was using the work in the sense of a carnival, but the older English sense of 'rout' was rather different, a fact gleefully taken up by *The Times* in its review of 17 December 1920:

At a chamber concert given at 139 Piccadilly (by permission of Baroness d'Erlanger) on Wednesday night, a new work called 'Rout' by Arthur Bliss was given a first performance. One hardly knows whether to describe it as chamber music or programme music, street music, or 'Jazz'. It has elements from them all. The cast begins like chamber music, and ends like orchestral music; mezzo-soprano voice, flute, clarinet, string quartet, double-bass, harp, side drum, and glockenspiel. The composer said that 'Rout' was used in the Old English sense, or one of the Old English senses. His was not Chaucer's sense … nor the 18th century sense of 'a fashionable evening assembly', but in the sense of a popular jollification, a Hampstead heathenish bank holiday rout. So the programme accounts for the street music and the 'Jazz' emerging from a number of rakish tunes for the voice, the clarinet, the flute and the strings tumbling over one another in wild confusion, while the double-bass cuts capers, the harp thrums accents, and the orchestral 'kitchen' behaves according to its kind. It is exceedingly clever, and proved quite captivating to an audience who belonged to the other kind of rout, the 'fashionable evening assembly'; they demanded and got its repetition. One has some misgivings about it however. Having heard several of these whimsical excursions one begins to wonder where they are lead-

Members of the Jury at the ISCM Festival, Winterthur, January 1926. Bliss is second from right and on his left are Arthur Honneger, the Swiss composer, and Edward Dent.

ing. Are they forming an individual style with which Mr Bliss will be able to say something when he has really got something to say, or is he becoming a fashionable joker? His abilities are much too good for the latter.[1]

Rout was an original conception which pre-dated *Façade* by two years and its natural charm was appreciated by Diaghilev, who asked Bliss to score it for full orchestra so that he could use it for intermissions between ballets, which probably helped to make the piece 'respectable' in the opinion of fashionable society. Another Bliss chamber work of the same year – *Conversations* – for a mixed string and woodwind quintet in five movements was equally clever but less successful, perhaps because its first public performance was at a concert in the Aeolian Hall when the programme also included music by three of the notorious 'Les Six'. These French composers, who included Milhaud and Poulenc, achieved this entirely unofficial title simply because they were all striving for new means of expression and were patronised by Stravinsky, who was also living in Paris; he declared himself to be 'excited only by the newest … and the youngest', a claim guaranteed to provoke notoriety for all concerned. But Bliss was not influenced by Les Six, nor even by Stravinsky for very long; he was just temporarily fascinated by them and their new tricks, especially Stravinsky's. He attempted, in 1921, to organize his thoughts about the 'new music' for an address to the Society of

1. *The Times*, 17 Dec 1920.

The front cover of the score of *Rout*, Bliss's controversial piece of 1920.

Women Musicians – 'What Modern Composition is Aiming At'[1] – which makes very interesting reading for anyone wanting to know how a young composer of the early 'twenties viewed the past, present and future of his chosen profession. More importantly in the context of this book, it gives a very clear picture of Bliss's personality at that time: his vitality, ease of expression and enthusiasm.

'I think enthusiasm is always welcome in these cynical days,' wrote Joseph Holbrooke. 'Any musician who comes to the front in Britain has to do it like a gentleman. They nearly all accomplish this; that is why I am intrigued with Arthur Bliss. Here is a semi-wild young man, who has perpetrated some singular and comic music, which has shocked a lot of people – and amused many. That is a distinct step in the right direction.'[2]

Rather a back-handed compliment, but Holbrooke was as eccentric as some of the people he wrote about and his thinly veiled distrust of Bliss's talents was mutual. He was referring not only to *Rout* and *Conversations* but also to *Madam Noy* – a setting (1918) of a quaint but previously unknown poem for soprano and six instruments – and *Rhapsody* (1919). The latter was another small chamber work for voices and instruments but in it the two voices were treated as additional instruments, singing the vowel sound *ah*. Bliss made it clear that in both these works he was merely experimenting with timbre, they were essays in the exploration of sound. The London critics, as a whole, tended to take them rather too seriously, searching primarily for meaning in the music, but one of them grasped the point precisely:

The clou of the evening was Arthur Bliss's 'Rhapsody' for two voices, flute, English horn and string quartet. Bliss has as yet produced little, but every work bears marks of a unique personality. His 'Rhapsody' is one of the few works precisely corresponding to that title, exquisitely coloured, but without preciousness or anaemic poeticism. Real poetry is there, however, of entrancing spirituality, a spirituality not produced by metaphysical pretensions, but by an intelligence which illuminates the rarest qualities of sensation and emotion, creating a glamour akin to Celtic legend ... But he is no vague visionary: he knows the value of instrumental timbre, and has a keen sense of fluid form. Above all, he is aware of that elusive quantity we term beauty. He is certainly a musician who counts.[3]

These early chamber works attracted some attention for their composer among the type of people who attended the evening salons of wealthy hostesses in London. His name was on the lips of pretty young flappers, who were always longing to be able to talk about the latest unconventional artist, writer or musician of the day; but could he spread this fame – or notoriety – to a wider

1. Bliss, op. cit. App 'A'.
2. Joseph Holbrooke, *Contemporary British Composers*, Cecil Palmer, 1925 pp161, 199.
3. Quoted by Bliss, op. cit. pp55-56.

'He knows the value of instrumental timbre …': the front cover of *Rhapsody*, another piece of 1920 which bore the '… mark of a unique personality'. Note that the composer 'corrected' the score of this early work over fifty years later.

audience? The chance came when he was asked to write music for a production of *The Tempest* at the Aldwych Theatre. The show was a strange mixture of styles in acting and design, a jumble which extended to the music – some Arne, some Sullivan, some Raymond Roze, some Frederick Norton and some Bliss. But out of all this mish-mash the critic Ernest Newman, who surprisingly attended, was able to highlight in his notice the music which had caught his ear:

The only music that matters is that of Mr Arthur Bliss, who, with a fearsome array of kettle-drums, has given us a storm in the opening scene that is not only terrifying in an imaginative way, instead of the merely noisy way of the old stage thunder, but has the additional and great merit of reducing the scenery and the actors to their native insignificance. For the scene in the fourth act, in which Prospero and Ariel and their satellites tease the ship-wrecked lords with a visionary table of delicacies, Mr. Bliss has written some music that I should like to hear again under more satisfactory conditions than those of the theatre. It has a strange remoteness and mystery: here one felt, as nowhere else, unfortunately, during the whole play after the storm scene, that Shakespeare's vision of an island enchanted had been realised. It is the most imaginative piece of theatre music that I have ever heard.[1]

To receive a notice like that by the pre-eminent music critic in the country, from such an unpromising genesis, must have seemed to Bliss like manna from heaven; it was exactly what he needed. Whether or not Elgar read this review is speculation but it was at the end of this year (1921) that he invited Bliss, Goossens and Howells to compose works for the Three Choirs Festival at Gloucester the following year, giving each of them the chance to write something big and significant. Bliss took it with both hands, but not before he had further interested the critics with another work. This was *Concerto for Piano, Tenor, Strings and Percussion*, in which the voice was again used instrumentally although singing 'abstract' words. All this experimenting with different vocal timbres gave the critics plenty of scope for jocularity:

I read that the concerto was to be regarded as pure abstract sound. Pure abstract sound! It may exist in the mind of God, but not in the Wigmore Hall on a Saturday afternoon, wrote one.[2]

But another took the piece rather more seriously:

A new concerto for piano and tenor voice was the central work in the programme of music for chamber orchestra which Mr Arthur Bliss conducted at the Wigmore Hall on Saturday.

This we take to be one of his recent compositions, and, if so, it is good evidence that he is not degenerating, as we have occasionally feared, into a mere musical 'stuntist'. For, whatever may be its defects, there is genuine music in the work. It is true that it rests on the perverse idea of using the voice as an instrument, and allowing it words merely as a means of securing the right sonorities. The words are not meant to be heard, and generally we did not hear them. This is irritating at first; afterwards one feels almost ashamed of having caught such a phrase as 'triumphing still, man shall endure', and it is difficult to pass it by without attaching any particular importance to it. But we are told that we must; 'there is no programme and no literary reason for employing the combination of voice, pianoforte, strings, and percussion'. So we tried dutifully to accept the composer's standpoint and to listen only to the music which Miss Myra Hess, Mr. Stewart Wilson, and the orchestra combined to make, not to one more than to another, and least of all to thoughts of man's endurance. And there was plenty to listen to. Apart from certain wilful excrescences of sound, the music moves through finely impulsive ideas with strong contrasts of mood and yet preserves

1. Quoted in Bliss, op. cit. p64.
2. Quoted in Bliss, op. cit. p66.

identity by thematic development. One does not catch the composer waiting for his next idea and filling in the blank spaces with mere antics. It is substantial music, and it was received with what seemed like genuine enjoyment by the large audience.'[1]

Bliss, however, made up his own mind that this particular experiment had not succeeded and rescored the work for two pianos and orchestra, the original score being lost during World War II when a bomb destroyed the warehouse where it and others were stored.

In October of that year, Bliss was given the chance by Henry Wood to conduct the première of a new work – his *Mêlée Fantasque* for full orchestra – at a Promenade concert in the Queen's Hall. His affection for, and gratitude to, Wood are evident in this extract from a talk he gave on BBC radio many years later:

In the years following the First World War it was very difficult for young composers, young singers, young players to get a chance to show what they could do. There were no powerful recording companies or broadcasting orchestras to help them. We all looked primarily to Henry Wood ...
I have spoken of Henry Wood's generosity, and this was plainly shown by the way he gave young musicians all possible time for rehearsal. In those days the Promenade Concerts had just one orchestra and one conductor. It was a real tour de force to get through the season – just the morning rehearsal for the evening concert. Henry Wood would skimp the time for the classical symphony and other repertoire works, to allow the young composer or the young soloist a really generous slice of the morning's rehearsal. In the evening, I remember waiting nervously to go on, and Henry Wood, as he did to so many others, would utter a word of encouragement, and then say, 'Wait a minute, till I get to my seat in the circle: I want to hear this.' That was a tonic for one's nerves.[2]

But now he had to fulfil his intention of composing, for the first time, a full-scale symphony for a large orchestra 'out of the blue', so to speak, and he had only a few months in which to do it. In his autobiography, he painted a very self-revealing picture of what it is like to sit before a blank sheet of manuscript paper, searching fruitlessly for inspiration, explaining how much he felt the need for some outside stimulus (words, a dramatic setting, a colourful occasion or the collaboration of a great performer) to help him begin. This sort of 'kick-start' remained a necessity to him through all the years when he was composing 'pure' – as opposed to 'dramatic' music; the abstract as opposed to the referential. For this new symphony, he eventually found the 'kick-start' in a chance perusal of a technical work on heraldry which described the symbolic associations of primary colours with heraldic design. Bliss translated this objective process into the

1. *The Times*, 12 June 1921.
2. *Bliss On Music*, p270 (from a talk broadcast on BBC Radio on 2 March 1969).

much more general and entirely subjective idea of attaching colour-tags to emotions; thus his first section/movement – deliberate and majestical in mood – was labelled, by him, with the colour purple.

The work was originally entitled 'Symphony in B' but Bliss was persuaded by the musicologist Percy Scholes, author of the Oxford Companion to Music, to call it *A Colour Symphony* and under that title it has become one of his most popular works, despite a troubled first performance at Gloucester Cathedral when the organizers got into a muddle with the seating and removed several of the poor conductor's key players from the platform just as he was about to begin.[1] The critical notices in the papers were unexpectedly favourable:

Bliss's Symphony marks a new stage in his career, an important one, because the first thing which must impress everyone is its earnestness. Some time ago it seemed an open question whether Bliss, with all his talents and facility, would develop as a serious composer, or be content to play with the resources of modern instrumental tone-colour and do little things for the astonishment of those who feed on astonishment. The Concerto seemed to me, at any rate, to show that he was out for the bigger thing; this Symphony leaves no doubt about it. Whether the title, 'A Colour Symphony', and the description of the four movements as purple, red, blue, and green, is a happy way of bringing his hearers into touch with him is an open question. For my own part, I found myself referring to the programme to find out whether I ought to be seeing red or looking blue at certain moments, and some of it certainly made many of the audience feel green.

But though he has chosen, or been persuaded, to tell something of his scheme of moods by the analogy of colour, the thing does not rest on any finicking illustrative idea. It is a symphony in its strong, melodic outlines and its processess of contrasted episodes. Its form is severely logical, granting its premises, and the last movement, of an elaborately-developed fugal type, is as strict as such things can be expected to be. Clear diatonic melodies spring forward at times, and have definite characters of their own. The harmonies – or should we call them conflicts? – of parts have the feeling of inevitability; they are certainly no affectation.

One feels that a razor-edge mind is at work, a young mind because it despises weakness and sentiment, and it is there, probably, that Bliss still has some growing-up to do. The music never seemed to appeal in the sense of wanting sympathy or giving it. Where it struck me as beautiful, as in the latter part of the first movement and the middle theme of the third, it was a cold beauty, and I felt all the time that what I liked best might be something on which the composer set comparatively little store. Probably the work was not altogether performed to the satisfaction of Bliss, who directed it (such first productions rarely are), but it is worth while to add that the orchestration all came out with extraordinary clearness. There was no difficulty in following the detail in even the most complex passages.[2]

1. Bliss describes this awful moment with his customary restraint in *As I Remember*, p73.
2. *The Times*, 8 Sept. 1922.

The work was dedicated to Adrian Boult who, sixty years later, wrote:

'I am very proud that my name has been written on the title page of 'The Colour Symphony'.'[1]

Bliss had been abroad with Boult several times to conduct concerts of British music – Amsterdam in 1920, Prague and Vienna two years later – and they formed a close association which did much to promote our native music in Europe and in America. Each admired the other's talents and they collaborated harmoniously throughout the rest of their working lives.

Returning to *The Colour Symphony*, although it comes early in Bliss's total output the work contains much of his characteristic style and because of this it might be the best one to study closely if one wished to appreciate his music better. He said that it was difficult to play and very intricate to conduct, but that was in the context of its first performance. Henry Wood seemed to have no complaint when he performed it at the Queen's Hall six months later. It is both romantic (in its slow movement – BLUE) and classical (in its finale – GREEN); it is strongly rhythmical (in its scherzo – RED) and ceremonial (in its opening movement – PURPLE). All these four elements typify the core of Bliss's mode of expression; they occur repeatedly, either singly or collectively, in all his music. Harmonically, it is dissonant in places and some chords grate on the ear even to-day but, as the composer himself nostalgically observed nearly fifty years after writing it, the sounds we found savage in our youth sound comparatively tame in old age. It is a work which will live because it stems from 'the glory of youth' and yet stands firm in the light of mature judgement.

A final question relating to this symphony remains: it was written in response to an invitation from Elgar, we know, but what did Elgar think of it? Bliss said that an estrangement had grown up between them since the first performance of the work in 1922 and quoted a letter from the older man (dated 8 November 1928) expressing disappointment in his progress 'from years ago' because of notoriety which had been reflected in the press and because he thought Bliss seemed to have become 'a mere paragraphist'.[2] The letter also implies that Bliss was a wealthy dilettante who didn't care if his compositions were commercially viable or not.

This could have been exceedingly hurtful and many weaker characters would have taken permanent offence. But Bliss's response was absolutely typical of the man: he wrote to ask Elgar to accept the dedication of another work he had just composed (the 'Pastoral', to be discussed later) and received a gracious acceptance in reply. It is not certain, however, whether Bliss was right in thinking that Elgar's huff was caused by the Symphony;

1. Boult, *RCM Magazine*.
2. Bliss, op. cit. p94.

according to Eugene Goossens, Elgar 'immensely admired it', whereas one of his biographers states 'At the Gloucester Festival in September 1922, the invitations to Bliss and Goossens resulted in works which Edward did not like.'[1] The important point is that whatever caused the estrangement, Bliss cured it in the most dignified way possible, and was delighted to have done so. About seven years after the first publication of the *Colour Symphony* in 1924 Bliss made substantial revisions and the final score was re-printed (by Hawkes & Son) in 1939. This was an early example of the composer's professional attitude to his music; he said that not only was his first review of a completed work better than the original but his second, third, fourth reviews were all better than the previous ones; self criticism was an endearing – and enduring – part of his personality and professionalism.

No sooner was this symphony launched into the public domain than Bliss left England for America. His father had married again in 1918 and now decided to return to live in his native country with most of his family (his second wife had two children of her own and a new daughter of her second marriage). It must have been a wrench for Arthur to leave England at the very moment when his career appeared to have made such a promising start but there is no hint of complaint about this in his account of the event. The family moved from place to place in the States until at last settling in Santa Barbara, California, on the Pacific coast about a hundred miles north-west of Los Angeles. There Mr Bliss bought a house in Montecito, which was to be his home until he died, aged 84, in 1930.

No doubt Arthur felt the main purpose of his long journey had been accomplished once his father was settled, so after a short while he 'escaped' to New York and later Boston, where he had the interesting experience of hearing Pierre Monteux putting the Boston Symphony Orchestra through their paces in a performance of his *Colour Symphony*. This was enlightening, first because of the brilliance of the players – their virtuosity – and secondly because of the advice Monteux gave him, to make his notation as simple as possible; intricate scoring, advised the great conductor, might look clever but was a curse to the players. He also went to Philadelphia to attend a Stokowski concert which he compared unfavourably with that of Monteux – the one driven, the other coaxed.

Returning to Santa Barbara, he spent his time teaching, conducting, composing, and even taking part in amateur dramatics. The sequel is described by one of his new relatives, his step-brother Patrick Mahony:

My mother married the American-born father of Arthur Bliss after my own father was killed in World War One. Mr Francis E. Bliss was the head of a large American firm in London and was a Victorian type of

1. J.N. Moore, op. cit p761.

gentleman with great culture and personal charm. In an age of sub-missive children he allowed Arthur to pursue his bent for music and cooperated in every way to make him the success that he is, although he would have preferred that his son take up medicine.

My step-father brought my mother, my sisters and I to the US in 1923, and Arthur came too. We were in search of a place where Mr Bliss could pass his declining years in a salubrious climate, and after a brief stay in Santa Barbara, California, Arthur insisted that this was it. His ador-ing father was anxious to settle where Arthur would wish to remain nearby, so a suitable home was purchased with special studio facilities for composing.

Arthur did some composing in Santa Barbara, including a string quartet, piano pieces, a song-cycle 'The Women of Yueh' which was per-formed locally by Eva Gautier. He gave lectures and also indulged in amateur dramatics, playing leads in Shaw's 'You Never Can Tell' and 'Beggar on Horseback' by Connelly and Kauffman, on which last occasion he met first the woman who played opposite to him who later became his wife, Miss Gertrude Hoffmann. She was the daughter of a local schoolmaster and botanist and belonged to a well-known family whom Arthur's father liked immensely.

Always gifted with the magic of attracting round his orbit fascinating personalities, Arthur was visited at this time by Sir Henry Wood and Sir Donald Tovey separately, and he became acquainted with some of the film luminaries, notably Alla Nazimova and Charles Chaplin. The latter advised Arthur that his plans to write classical music for the films were premature and that they would mature only when moving pictures would be taught to talk. But Arthur conducted one of his major works for the Hollywood Bowl, a piece which was not well received because it was considered too modern.

Thus discouraged by other hopes frustrated, Arthur decided to take his wife to London and settle there, much to the regret of us all, especially his father who loved him deeply. They did meet again at a New York resort but never in Santa Barbara. My step-father died in 1931 [sic] at Santa Barbara.

As a step-brother I remember him as fairly understanding (I was twelve, he thirty-two) and kindly if sometimes sarcastic. As a boy, I admired his magnetic charm, his wit and whimsical wisdom, the firm-ness with which he grasped the cord of life. Even then his indefatigable vigour, the strenuous activity of his intellect, and the breadth of his sympathies pointed him out to me as someone outstanding. Success to some extent he had already enjoyed in England, But I believe his Santa Barbara days, with the contrast of scene and way of life, affected his musical language favourably, making it more mellifluous, more balanced and burnished and perhaps more perfected in its technical softness and smoothness. This is borne out in his 'Hymn to Apollo', which he sketched out before he returned to London and which was performed soon afterwards.[1]

1. 'Sir Arthur Bliss: 75th Birthday', reproduced with kind permission of the Composers' Guild of Great Britain, from *Composer* No20 Summer 1966. *Note*: Lady Bliss has told me that the first of *Three Romantic Songs* ('The Hare') which her husband com-posed in 1921, was dedicated to his step-brother, Patrick Mahony, the second song ('Love Locks') was dedicated to his step-sister and the third ('The Buckle') to his half-sister.

The wedding of Arthur and Trudy at Santa Barbara, California, in 1925.

The *Hymn to Apollo* is not, in fact, a hymn in the generally accepted sense because it is written for full orchestra, has no voices, and lasts for about eleven minutes. Bliss called it an invocation to Apollo as the god of the art of healing and it does have the character of a prayer, with its pleading phrases at the start and its tremendous climax near the end. An interesting point in Mr Mahony's account is that this piece was evidently conceived in America, during the time of the composer's courtship of his future wife, and not back in London two years later when it is generally thought to have been started. It might, therefore, have had romantic associations but the music contains no such clues.

However, as with *A Colour Symphony*, Bliss wrote a new version of the piece many years later (1964) and it is in this revised form that it is now recorded. Bliss states that he conducted the first performance at a Queen's Hall Prom in September 1926, and that Monteux played it in Amsterdam two months later; he adds:

Through my life I have suffered the disadvantage that conductors have only known the original score, and ... failed to renew their interest with my final and revised editions.[1]

Perhaps, in view of the high and dramatic quality of *Hymn to Apollo* and the convenient length, programme-planners of to-day would be well rewarded by giving it consideration, in its revised version.

The wedding of Arthur and Trudy at Santa Barbara on 1st June 1925 was the culmination of a romantic courtship and engagement which took place in idyllic surroundings – perfumed lemon groves bordering the Pacific, the desert of Southern California and the foothills of mysterious mountains, peach and apricot blossom in the spring, scores of poppies after the rains – they are all described (in *As I Remember*) in the vivid colours of youth in love, though written when the marriage was over forty years on.

After a short honeymoon, the couple came to London where they rented a flat in Redcliffe square. The sudden change of environment for Trudy Bliss, who had never been to England before, must have been disturbing, to say the least, but she insists that she did not feel lonely or isolated – 'it was simply exchanging one family environment for another' – and her husband was at once welcomed back by the friends he had left two years before, among whom were R.O. Morris and his wife Jane. Morris was Vaughan Williams's brother-in-law and shared a house with him and his wife in Cheyne Walk, where Bliss had previously had a room in which he began composing his *Colour Symphony*. Now into this select little musical coterie, plus a few literary friends, came Trudy, the attractive-looking and highly intelligent American girl with her unaffected charm and poise: the effect must have been rather sensational. She was soon taking lessons

1. Bliss, op. cit. p90.

in musical theory with Morris at the Royal College of Music, where Bliss also taught for a while, and meeting other prominent musicians such as Harriet Cohen the pianist. The process of re-establishing themselves in London's artistic circles had begun; but, more important, the invaluable part played by Trudy Bliss in gracing and furthering the career of her husband was also under way.

Bliss's career, however, was at a watershed. He had written a score of works, only one of them – the symphony – of any considerable length, and he was still uncertain whether his future lay in England or in America. He dedicated his next orchestral work *Introduction and Allegro*, completed in June 1926 (revised 1937), to Leopold Stokowski and the Philadelphia Orchestra; the following summer he and Trudy, with their one-year-old daughter Barbara, were off again to Santa Barbara to show her to her grandfather.

While in the States Arthur met Mrs Elizabeth Sprague Coolidge, the great American patroness of chamber music, and this was a fortunate encounter: she asked him to write a work for Leon Goossens to play at her festival of chamber music due to take place in Venice in the autumn of that same year. He must have worked quickly when they returned to London, because the *Quintet for Oboe and Strings* (dedicated to Mrs Coolidge) was ready for performance by Goossens and the Venetian String Quartet on 11 September, repeated soon afterwards in Vienna. Bliss and his wife, with Mrs Coolidge in tow (or should it be the other way round?) motored from one city to another, finally ending up in Amsterdam.

In the spring of the following year, 1928, the Blisses were off again, this time to Sicily for a holiday with some American friends, but work was not far from Arthur's mind. He had recently met Harold Brooke, a director of the publishers Novello's, who had asked him to write a choral work for a small mixed choir in London which he conducted. Bliss found the inspiration for this commission during the Sicilian holiday. Trudy Bliss sets the scene:

'Now into this select little musical coterie ... came Trudy ... the effect must have been rather sensational'; Trudy Bliss in London, ten years after her marriage.

For two weeks we roamed round Sicily, Etna menacing us behind Taormina, and in the garden of Taormina were the largest violets I had ever seen and narcissus in blossom so early in the year. The mimosa and the jasmine and the nostalgic scent from the lemon orchards, all took us back to Santa Barbara. And our last stop was Agrigento, where there is a famous cluster of ruined Greek temples in a little sheltered valley. We sat more than one morning on the steps of the biggest temple, the Temple of Juno, and in the sweet spring grass, beyond the steps was a great flock of sheep and goats. And, though he was out of sight, very clearly came the sounds of the shepherd's pipe.[1]

---

1. From a talk given by Lady Bliss to choirs when they were going to perform the *Pastoral;* with permission.

The temple of Juno at
Agrigento.

Arthur himself presents a slight variation of this backdrop:

It was at this latter place [Syracuse], when one morning I had set out to
explore the site of the classical fountain of Arethusa, a copy of the 'Idylls'
of Theocritus in my pocket, that I found the theme for my choral work.[1]

Bliss called the work *Pastoral – Lie strewn the white flocks*,
the sub title being a line from a poem by Matthew Arnold
('Empedocles on Etna') although this is not used in the text, which
is an anthology of verse from different epochs, a device which he
used again in his next choral work (*Morning Heroes*). All the poems
evoke an arcadian atmosphere and, in the compiler's words,
'depict a Sicilian day from dawn to evening'. But it is the music
which brings the scene into focus and enhances the poetry with
life, especially in the well known 'Pigeon Song', a solo for mezzo-
soprano which is sometimes performed separately (a pity in some
ways because it is more effective in context). The whole work,
which lasts just over half an hour, is one of the most delightful in
the repertoire for small choir and orchestra; it is also within the
capabilities of good amateur singers and players.
    The dedication to Elgar, already mentioned, and its first per-
formance (which was broadcast) prompted a letter from him
addressed to 'Dear Bliss' in which he admitted that he had listened
to it on the wireless under conditions 'far from good' but nevertheless they had enabled him to judge that the piece was 'on a

1. Bliss, op. cit. p93.

46

The great American
patroness of chamber music
– Elizabeth Sprague Coolidge
– herself an accomplished
pianist and composer – a
portrait by Sargent.

large and *fine* scale' – adjectives which could hardly be less accurate – and that he liked it *'exceedingly'*.[1]

The work also had a powerful effect on Harold Brooke of Novello's which was of lasting value. From that time, almost all the music Bliss wrote was published by that firm, and a close friendship ensued with Brooke. His small office was at the back of the large building which the company inhabited in Wardour Street and there he achieved his meticulous editing which Bliss so much appreciated. He also valued his advice, given at rehearsals of his works which Brooke regularly attended. Presentation copies of each new work, bound in leather, were given to the composer and the firm even printed his Christmas cards, in a specially designed format.[2]

After the first performance of *Pastoral*, Bliss made another visit to America to see his father and on his return began composing his *Serenade* for baritone and orchestra, a setting of an anthology of poems in the style of an eighteenth-century vocal serenata. The inspiration came on this occasion from a picture he saw in a gallery – possibly by Fragonard – depicting a lover singing songs of courtship in a romantic setting, with temples, grottos and all the accompaniments of that pleasure-loving age. It was first performed at one of the Courtauld-Sargent concerts at the Queen's Hall and Bliss dedicated it to his wife.

By this time, they had moved from the studio flat in Redcliffe Square to East Heath Lodge, Hampstead, a substantial house 'with a splendid view', in which Bliss had a work-room on the first floor. Although the doors were shut and the walls thick, the piano – at which he always composed – could be clearly heard. Many times his wife paused as she walked up or down stairs to wonder what the next work was going to be, but soon she was invited into the studio to have it played and described as it progressed.[3]

The sounds she heard during that summer of 1929 were the beginnings of her husband's largest work since the *Colour Symphony* – a choral symphony written to expurgate the memories of the trenches on the Western Front in the War. Bliss describes (in *As I Remember* p96) how he still suffered from a nightmare in which he believed he and a few others had been forgotten and abandoned to continue the battle against the enemy – similarly forgotten – and doomed to fight on until extinction. This horror, together with the memory of his dead brother, impelled him to complete a work which would finally exorcise his distressing experiences. *Morning Heroes* is a long symphony (it lasts for about an hour) for orator, chorus and orchestra in five movements, only the last of which relates specifically to the war which Bliss had experienced, the first four being concerned with various aspects of war in general: first, the parting of husband and wife (scene

1. Bliss, op. cit. p95.
2. From a note kindly supplied by Lady Bliss.
3. Ibid.

An example of the Christmas cards printed by Novello.

and text from Homer's *Iliad*); second, the army being recruited and trained (Walt Whitman's poem 'Drum Taps'); third, the young wife left alone (an ancient Chinese poem) contrasted with her man on watch at the battlefield; and fourth, the heroes of the title (chosen by Bliss himself from Homer's illustrious dead). The final movement is the apotheosis of heroism in words by Wilfred Owen and Robert Nichols, set to music of almost unbearable emotional tension.

The work therefore focuses mainly on two aspects of war: the waste of young lives and the pity of it; secondly, the heroism of those involved in battle and, equally but differently, of those left at home. For three quarters of it, the listener is spared some of the sadness because the scene and text are far removed from the battlefields of France and Belgium in 1914-18 (unlike Britten's *War Requiem*, composed thirty years later, in which the sorrow is almost unrelieved), but in the last section we are alongside Bliss, the young soldier, and his brother, Kennard, facing those fearful guns, dodging the wicked blasts of shrapnel, squelching in the stinking mud and watching our friends being torn to pieces a few paces from us. The heroes, having been recognized from ancient legend, are now indistinguishable in the encircling mist, and Bliss's nightmare is enshrouded too and laid to rest.

The work was first performed at the Norwich Festival in October 1930, and the critics were mostly impressed:

The significant fact is that at last the composer has set himself in this music to reveal thoughts out of many hearts. He has a great deal to say.[1]

It is obvious that Mr Bliss has devised an excellent framework; there is nothing apparently defective in the plan of his work until the fifth part, the last movement of the symphony.[2]

1. *The Times*, 24 October 1930.
2. W.J. Turner, *Facing the Music*, G. Bell & Sons Ltd, London 1933, p16.

48

The Times' critic, W.J. Turner, had a little grumble about the use of the spoken voice – 'the musical substance taking a secondary place in the design' – before praising the final movement and even comparing its counterpoint with that of Bach:

There is great beauty in the development of one long orchestral tune. Before the finale, Wilfred Owen's 'Spring Offensive' is spoken by the Orator, with only the drums in a distant cannonade accompanying the voice. It leads to Robert Nichols' 'Dawn on the Somme', double chorus *quasi chorale*, with a wreathing figure of accompaniment begun on the wood-wind and joining itself more closely with the chorus as the words are reached, 'Oh! Is it mist, or are these companies of morning heroes who arise?' So the modern composer turns back to something not only of the form, but the spirit of Bach when he makes ending, and it is in these final pages that we realize that Arthur Bliss has made his great step forward and, in saying what is old, has said something new and true.[1]

However, Mr Turner took exception to this last section of the Symphony on the grounds that it was not part of a 'symphony' – that is, it did not synthesize with the rest of the work:

Here he has chosen a poem, Owen's 'Spring Offensive', which does not lend itself to musical treatment, and Mr Bliss has recognised this fact by having it declaimed by the orator. But the same is true of 'Hector's Farewell', which also is declaimed. On the other hand, Walt Whitman's words and 'Achilles goes forth to Battle' lend themselves perfectly to choral setting, and are accordingly so set. Having recognised this, it is strange that Mr Bliss has not perceived that these two groups do not and, I shall say, cannot coalesce. A 'symphony', a harmony, or consonance of sounds, is just what 'Morning Heroes' is not, because its parts are not musically related. If we examine Berlioz's works, such as the 'Symphony Fantastique' or 'Harold in Italy', where he has worked to a programme of literary inspiration, we will find that everything is achieved musically, and words are never – not even in the Faust music – allowed to pull their full weight or used as Mr Bliss uses them, for their own sake.[2]

The critic has here fastened on a problem which every composer who has set to music a vivid text has had to face: should the words dominate the progression of the music, on a rational basis, or should the music progress in a way appropriate to the words but not at their behest? And having decided that in this symphony Bliss has opted for the first alternative, and thus allowed the unity of the work to suffer (Owen's 'Spring Offensive', he argues, does not – cannot – 'coalesce' with the other poems used) he concedes that this would be a pedantic objection if the music itself had been enjoyable and effective:

1. *The Times*, 24 October 1930.
2. W.J. Turner, *Facing the Music*, G. Bell & Sons Ltd, London 1933 pp16-17.

Unfortunately I could find there nothing to admire or enjoy. The music is not only derivative, without anything fresh and individual, but it is not particularly effective, as Elgar, even in his banal moments, can be effective. In fact, I cannot help feeling that if Mr Bliss could listen to his music critically without all the literary associations he has connected with it, he would himself realise how far from his conception it has turned out to be.[1]

This was a harsh judgement on a work which has stood the test of time and which was, after all, an intensely *personal* creation. In a BBC Radio Three programme, broadcast on 9 November 1985, 'The Making of *Morning Heroes*', the fact of Arthur's deeply felt love for his brother Kennard and his profound shock at the news of his death is made painfully clear in the commentary. And perhaps we should also remember that the symphony was dedicated not only to the memory of Kennard but 'all other comrades killed in battle'; as George Dannatt wrote, Bliss 'sought to embrace what war has meant – and means – for all peoples everywhere, then, and now.'[2] This is a perspective view of the symphony which a critic in 1930 could not possibly have had. Finally, if the work is not, strictly speaking, a 'symphony' because it does not synthesize, as Turner says, we must ask what other description it merits. Bliss must have considered 'requiem' but abandoned it because of its liturgical cognation; he always thought deeply about the uses of words and their associated meanings, so we can be sure that as he called it a 'Symphony for Orator, Chorus and Orchestra', that is what he meant. Giles Easterbrook has found the best answer to Turner's criticism:

I have ... met only one description of the word [symphony] that holds good for all periods and styles, namely that a symphony is 'that form to which a composer naturally turns when expressing his most important or profound thoughts...' In all these 'Morning Heroes' emphatically qualifies.[3]

1. W.J. Turner, op. cit p17.
2. George Dannatt, Programme Notes for a performance of *Morning Heroes*, Festival Hall, London, 20 Nov 1985.
3. G. Easterbrook, Notes for Cala Records CD of *Morning Heroes*, 1992.

4 Between the Wars

The chair she sat in, like a burnished throne,
Glowed on the marble, where the glass ...
Doubled the flames of sevenbranched candelabra ...

T.S. Eliot – from 'A Game of Chess' ('The Waste Land')

Thought I heard the thunder rumbling in the sky;
It was Hitler over Europe, saying: 'They must die.'
O we were in his mind, my dear, O we were in his mind,

W.H. Auden – from 'Refugee Blues'

1930 was the start of the most productive decade in Arthur Bliss's composing career. Happily married and settled in a pleasant house in London, with one daughter already born (Barbara) and another (Karen) arriving shortly, he and Trudy were indeed fortunate. Only the deaths of both their fathers marred these early 1930s years: Mr Frank Bliss died at Santa Barbara in his eighty-fourth year and Mr Hoffmann died from an accident while on a botanical expedition, also in America.

Family bereavements might still have been in Arthur's mind while he was composing his *Quintet for Clarinet and Strings* completed in 1932, and his *Fanfare for Heroes* of the same year. The quintet is a lyrical work in which the clarinet's plaintive and sombre tones are more often heard than its puckish and sprightly ones (although these are exploited towards the end). The slow 'Adagietto expressivo' is one of Bliss's most heart-felt – and heart-touching – pieces of music; he must, surely, have still had his clarinettist brother, Kennard, in mind when he wrote it. Frederick Thurston and the Kutcher Quartet gave the first performance privately at East Heath Lodge and the first public one at the Wigmore Hall early the following year. Previously, the *Fanfare* had been performed at the Albert Hall in a concert in aid of the Musicians Benevolent Fund. It is one of over thirty such works composed by Bliss for various occasions and he is justly renowned as the master of this genre; although he told his friend, the critic and artist George Dannatt 'they don't take me long',[1] they are all – including those (three) written for the Investiture of the Prince of Wales at Caernarfon in 1969 – models of good taste and of good brass-orchestration. The Russian publicity experts must have concurred, because they chose to use *Fanfare*

1. George Dannatt, Intro. to 'Catalogue' of Complete Works (Foreman), Novello 1979, p15.

Lionel Tertis, pictured in the early 1930s at about the time he premièred Bliss's Viola Sonata. (Courtesy of Mrs L. Tertis)

for Heroes in a film about their soldiers defending Stalingrad in 1942.

The viola was regarded for many years by orchestral musicians as a bit of a joke; for one thing, the classical repertoire (except for that of Mozart, who played the instrument) does not give the viola section much interesting work – line after line of rather dull notes, very often – and it was unkindly suggested that players who could not manage to hold their places in the higher register of the violin section might find life less stressful by taking up the viola. Enter Lionel Tertis at about the turn of the century, and all that began to change. He had total dedication to his aim (to establish the viola as a solo instrument), large hands, and a very able commercial brain. He tells the story of his success – and the viola's – in his book, *My Viola and I*.[1] Perhaps he recognized in Arthur Bliss not only the quality of refined musicianship but also a touch of that dedicated aim and determination which he employed himself; it was not long after they became friends that he asked the composer for a sonata and the request was accepted. Goossens for the oboe quintet, Thurston for the clarinet quintet and now Tertis for a viola sonata: in his autobiography, Bliss makes no secret of the fact that he liked writing solo works for great players and, in fact, drew inspiration from the process. These great performers were only the beginning of a long list: – Solomon, Campoli, Ferrier, Rostropovitch – who asked for new music from him and fired his enthusiasm with their genius.

Once again, the first performance was a private one at East Heath Lodge (9 May 1933) 'to a very distinguished gathering of musicians, and I recall that William Walton turned the pages for us.'[2] Solomon was at the piano for this occasion and also for the Sonata's first public performance at a BBC chamber concert later in the year, but not long afterwards, in 1935, Rubinstein took Solomon's place at very short notice and, according to Tertis, read the very difficult piano part at sight at the rehearsal. It is worth mentioning that Bliss did not compose any more sonatas for two instruments, although he had written one for violin and piano in his early days (c1914) which was never published; the holograph is in the Cambridge University Library.

The Bliss house on the edge of Hampstead Heath had now witnessed the composition of the large scale *Morning Heroes* and the first performance of two chamber works, but Arthur and Trudy also wanted a retreat in the country, where they could take their young family during the summer, and where he could work undisturbed by visitors and telephones. After a long and fruitless search for such a place, they decided to build their own and found a large plot for sale in a wood near the Somerset village of Penselwood. Their architect-friend Peter Harland designed it and they watched the house going up with growing enthusiasm. 'Pen Pits',

1. Elek Books Ltd, London 1974.
2. Tertis, op. cit p74.

'A distinctive 1930s house ...' – 'Pen Pits' (designed by Peter Harland) nearing completion in the Autumn of 1934.

as it was called, emerged from a tangle of undergrowth and a mass of trees and saplings (the site had been an old forest, possibly used by King Alfred as a camp) and underneath all this were scores of deep circular cavities ('moon-like craters'[1]) which emphasized its ancient origin and some of which had to be levelled. To see a house – and a distinctive 1930s house at that – emerge, with the outline of a garden and even a distant view, from such a labyrinth must certainly have been an exciting experience for the owners. Not surprisingly, they made frequent visits from London while building progressed, 'longing to be part of it'[2] as Trudy says, until they knew that journey intimately:

... I remember those three-hour journeys by car to Pen Pits from East Heath Lodge. My husband and I used to take turns driving but whoever was not driving participated in the lovely game of I-Spy, where each animal encountered had a different points value, and I can remember one unexpected circus raising a shout of 'one elephant, 25 points to me'.

Also, daughter Barbara really liked memorising poetry and so she used to regale us with verse after verse of 'Horatius at the bridge'. 'Oh Tiber, Father Tiber ... Oh hear a Roman's prayer', or a bit from 'The Lady of Shalott', 'On either side the river lie long fields of barley and of rye'.

The family animals of course came with us backwards and forwards. Once I remember a beloved cat got out of its basket at the picnic stage,

1. Bliss, op. cit, p103/4.
2. Note from Lady Bliss.

disappeared into the bushes, refusing to come back when called and delayed us for over a frustrating hour. And a cocker spaniel cherished in the back seat between our knees.[1]

It was the kind of surroundings to which Elgar would have been attracted, had he seen it (shades of his song 'The Wanderer'[2]) but at the very time it was being built Elgar was dying and when the end came (February 1934) there was only passing interest in the national press, for the composer of *Gerontius* had survived into an age which he neither understood nor liked. The rough, hard sounds of 'modern' music were anathema to him and although he had tried – in the *Quintet for Piano and Strings* for example – to reach forward and grasp the new idiom, it was music fashioned by an 'old' man, with a sigh of resignation. There is no mention of his death in *As I Remember*, but Bliss kept his letters and in the address he gave in Worcester on the centenary date of Elgar's birth (5 June 1957) his eulogy leaves no doubt at all about his feelings:

For me the predominant effect of Elgar's music is an enhancement of life. That is why I give thanks for the appearance in England of this great composer; that is why I rejoice to celebrate his genius during this week; and that is why I believe that, after fine performances of his music, we emerge better, stronger, and more sensitive human beings.[3]

At this time there was another novelty on the horizon for Arthur Bliss. Following a chance meeting with H.G. Wells, he was asked to compose the music for a proposed film based on Wells's book, *The Shape of Things to Come*. He responded with typical enthusiasm to this new challenge but with his eyes fully open to the danger; he knew little in detail about the technique of making films at this stage but he was aware that producers and their assistants were liable to cut a lot of the score if it was composed before the cutting process began; similarly, large parts of it might be rejected entirely when the several sound-tracks were combined into one (dubbing). If he did not fully appreciate the harrowing effects of these drastic processes on author and composer at the outset, he was made aware of them by Wells, who, in a forthright letter to him in October,[4] hatched a plan to overcome these difficulties as far as possible.

The film-making technique had, of course, been absorbed from America, indeed from Hollywood, very near the district which Bliss knew so well, but apart from a few brief encounters with some of the 'stars' (eg Chaplin), Bliss had not had the opportunity to study the technique over there. Most of the established American film-composers were quite used to having their scores mauled and slashed during production but for a novice it could be a sad experience – for example, Stravinsky was employed by

1. Note from Lady Bliss.
2. J.N. Moore, op. cit. p765.
3. *Bliss on Music* (Ed. Roscow) p247.
4. Bliss, op. cit. p104.

Things to Come – a scene from the film, 1936.
(Photo, National Film Archive)

Columbia in 1940 to write the music for a war-film, *Commandos Strike at Dawn*. When he had completed it, having heard the story of the film, a play-through was arranged at the studio. Yes, they said, the music was fine but unfortunately it didn't fit the film – so good-bye Mr Stravinsky! He is said to have gone away 'perplexed', although he was able to use the music later for a concert-piece.[1]

Bliss was wiser in following the dictum of another film composer, Erich Korngold, who wrote:

Music is music, whether it is for the stage, the rostrum or the cinema ... The cinema is a direct avenue to the ears and hearts of the great public, and all musicians should see the screen as a musical opportunity.[2]

Bliss acknowledged later that although the making of *Things to Come* had many fascinations for him, many modifications had to be made to his score – a delightful and typical euphemism. In fact, it was Wells himself who, in the end, became disillusioned with the film; he had hoped it would spread the serious warning of mass destruction by modern weapons to a much wider audience than his book could do but, in the making, the film became just another entertainment – albeit an exciting one – and thus it contributed to the writer's increasing pessimism about mankind's future.

Bliss was also fortunate in having Muir Mathieson as musical director at the Denham Studio, a pleasant and highly efficient

1. See Tony Thomas, *Music for the Movies*, A. S. Barnes & Co, Tantivy Press, London 1973, p42.
2. Ibid, quoted on p19. Korngold (1897-1957) wrote the music for his first film, *Captain Blood*, in 1935.

55

colleague who made the 'fatiguing and anxious job' of fitting his music to the film much more tolerable than it might have been. How much of what he originally wrote was 'wasted' in the process is not important because he was able to use all he wanted in a concert suite published by Novello after the film was released. This suite was, and still is, very popular with audiences, especially the famous 'March' with which it ends. Other versions of the suite were made by various arrangers for a smaller orchestra, military band, brass band and piano.

Whatever lingering doubts Bliss may have had about *Things to Come*, did not deter him from writing five more film scores over the years: *Conquest of the Air* was composed in 1937 and the film released three years later, the subsequent suite being dedicated by Bliss to Muir Mathieson who conducted its first performance. In 1944, Bernard Shaw asked him to collaborate in a film version of his play *Caesar and Cleopatra*; he wrote two letters to Bliss which bubble over with Shavian meddlesomeness and wit:

In Heaven's name, no Egyptian music. It must not even be sham Egyptian: it would be sham 'Aida'. It must be Blissful and British ...[1]

Arthur Bliss wrote later that he started on a 'skeleton piano score' but, having met the director of the film (Gabriel Pascal) he decided to withdraw from the project. In fact, there are eighty-four pages of unpublished manuscript[2] which cover ten items in the film in full score, so the 'skeleton' became rather more like an Egyptian mummy. The following year (1945) he composed music for *Men of Two Worlds*, another British film but released in America with the title: *Kisenga, Man of Africa*. The main item is a piano piece, with orchestra and male voices, called 'Baraza'; this was played for the film by Eileen Joyce, again with Mathieson conducting. 'Baraza' was written out by Bliss as a concert item but not published; on the manuscript it is explained that the title means 'a discussion between an African Chief and his head men'.[3] He later arranged it as a piece for two pianos and this was published by Novello in 1946. Bliss's remaining two film scores – *Christopher Columbus* (1949) and *Seven Waves Away* (*Abandon Ship* in America) which was written in 1956 – are unpublished and the holographs, in the Cambridge University Library, are incomplete; a suite from the former was arranged by Marcus Dods but has not as yet been published.[4]

Bliss was convinced that the experience of writing music for films was beneficial to the composer's art:

I have written several scores for films ... and I am sure the discipline involved is good for a composer's technique. It certainly teaches him the value of the blue pencil, of having to delete whole bars, sew up the

1. Quoted in Bliss, op. cit. p167.
2. Cambridge University Library.
3. Stewart Craggs *Arthur Bliss – A Source Book*, Scolar Press 1996 p129.
4. Ibid, p84.

passage neatly to an exact timing, and express his thoughts in an aphoristic form. It is salutary to see how often compression improves the music. Not always, of course: there are certain works whose nature demands leisure and space, but quite a number (and one can tell this from an audience's sudden relaxation) outstay their welcome; ending punctually is one of the marks of the great masters.[1]

But after completing the score of *Things to Come* in 1934, he may have felt instinctively that his next work should be a piece of 'pure' music which would allay any suspicion that he was not a 'serious' composer. There was, indeed, among some critics a snobbish element, both in Britain and in America, which considered film-scoring a futile occupation for a 'serious' composer and refused to take anything written subsequently at face value. Bliss's perceptive intuition about such matters now came to his aid, not for the first or last time, and in the following year he composed *Music for Strings* for the Salzburg Festival at which Boult gave the first performance with the Vienna Philharmonic Orchestra; not only were the players and the venue distinguished, the audience included Toscanini, Weingartner and Bruno Walter! Bliss himself was present and reported to his wife, in a letter written immediately afterwards, that the work had been well received and he had acknowledged the applause 'three times from the balcony' adding 'I wish you had been there, next time I shall take you, money or no'.[2]

This is an appropriate place to pause and consider for a moment the often-asked question, was Arthur Bliss a 'romantic' composer? Incidentally, Bliss himself posed the question in his autobiography at this point in his career. The answer he gave was that although *Music for Strings* is a 'neutral title', it *is* a romantic work because creative art itself is a romantic urge and 'music is the romantic art par excellence.'[3] This neat explanation, with a hint of irony, is a typical 'Blissism' because it adroitly avoids a definition of 'romantic' but at the same time applies the word to this particular composition. Early in 1934, before embarking on *Things to Come*, he had given a series of three lectures at the Royal Institution on 'Aspects of Contemporary Music' which naturally refer to music written in the immediate post-war period, but they are very well worth reading to-day (see *Bliss on Music*, pages 69-104) because of the light they throw on his opinions about such matters as 'creativity', 'emotion' and thence – 'romanticism'. One quotation, although failing to do justice to the series as a whole, might help a reader who cannot spare the time to read them all:

Let me here sum up my creed. I believe that the foundation of all music is emotion, and without the capacity for deep and subtle emotion a composer only employs half the resources of his medium. I believe that

1. Bliss, op. cit. p106.
2. Bliss, op. cit p109.
3. Bliss, op. cit. p108.

this emotion should be called into being by the sudden awareness of actual beauty seen, or by the vision of beauty vividly apprehended. I believe that the emotion resulting from apprehended beauty should be solidified and fixed by presenting it in a form absolutely fitting to it, and to it alone. If I were to define my musical goal, it would be to try for an emotion truly and clearly felt, and caught for ever in a formal perfection.[1]

In the autumn of 1935, AB (as his friends called him) was commissioned by the *Listener* – a BBC publication – to undertake a musical survey of Britain, similar in some respects to his friend Priestley's social survey (*English Journey*), published in the previous year. Bliss was immensely interested in the idea because it would allow him to discover the 'lesser-known' musical activities of his own country outside London: he was referring to choirs, instrumental groups large and small, music in schools, colleges and clubs, amateur operatic societies and all those non-professional or semi-professional organisations which flourished in local areas but hardly ever received a mention in the national press. He wanted to find out *inter alia* what opportunities there were for music students in large towns miles from London, and whether broadcasting was helping or hindering the various musical activities he expected to discover.

It was an ambitious project (no survey is ever thoroughly complete) and an exhausting one (he travelled about two-and-a-half-thousand miles in three months) but the published result, in twelve parts,[2] makes fascinating reading. This was partly because AB's enquiring mind led him to ask the right sort of questions to the people most likely to know the answers, and also because his own music, from this year onwards, was influenced by his experience (his Brass Band compositions, for example, began with the suite *Kenilworth*, written for the Crystal Palace Brass Band Championships in 1936). Again, there is space for only one quotation (from the 'Conclusion', published in the *Listener* of 18 December 1935):

It is indeed the quantity of music everywhere that has most astonished me. There seems hardly a village which is not touched by some musical organization. In a general way broadcasting has been the most potent cause of this growth. It has awakened the sense of music in vast sections of the population. There is naturally a percentage of this new audience who are lazily content to take the ready-made article as handed to them, but there are other listeners who wish to get in closer touch with music by learning to take part themselves. I believe it can be proved by statistics that many more are learning to play instruments or are keen to join musical societies now than in the pre-broadcasting days. This statement rests on the result of discussions with professional teachers of music in widely separated parts of the country.[3]

1. *Bliss on Music*, op. cit. p100.
2. *Bliss on Music*, op. cit. pp105-155.
3. *Bliss on Music*, op. cit. p152.

The 'pilgrimage', as he called it, gave him personal experience
of a wide variety of musical activity in the country and of a cross-
section of the people involved in it. His contacts with some of
these people are sympathetically and humorously described in *As
I Remember*,[1] and he proved to himself – if any proof was needed
– that he could rapidly make friends with anyone from any social
group, especially when music was the common interest. Evidence
of the wide appeal both of his music and of his musical personality
is shown in two letters,[2] one from a Brass Band musician and the
other from a monk (see illustrations).

Bliss was fortunate in possessing a spontaneous sense of
humour – especially a sense of the absurd – tempered by a ready
sympathy with people who were honestly trying to play or sing
his music to the best of their ability. Both these qualities would

1. See for example, p111.
2. By permission of Lady Bliss.

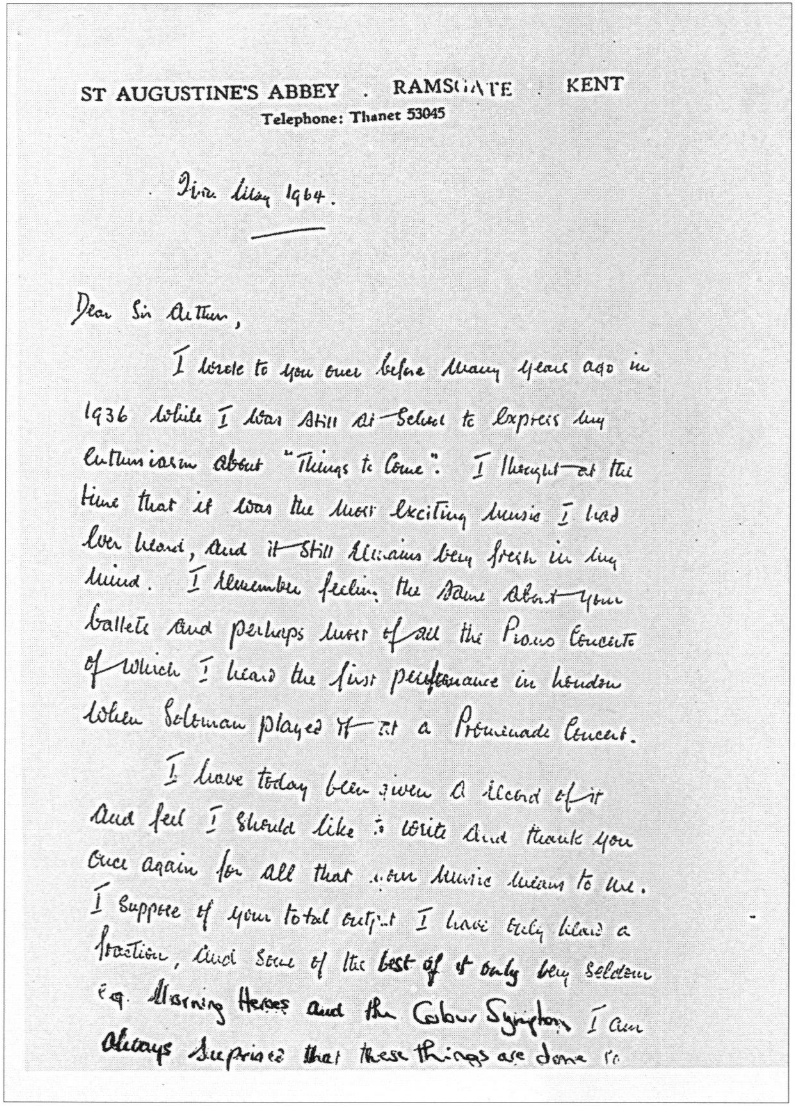

ST AUGUSTINE'S ABBEY · RAMSGATE · KENT
Telephone: Thanet 53045

13th May 1944.

Dear Sir Arthur,

I wrote to you once before many years ago in 1936 whilst I was then at school to express my enthusiasm about "Things to Come". I thought at the time that it was the most exciting music I had ever heard, and it still strikes me very fresh in my mind. I remember feeling the same about your ballet and perhaps most of all the Piano Concerto of which I heard the first performance in London when Solomon played it — at a Promenade Concert.

I have today been given a record of it and feel I should like to write and thank you once again for all that more music means to me. I suppose if you're total output I have truly heard a fraction, and even some of the best of it only very seldom (e.g. Morning Heroes and the Colour Symphony I am always surprised that these things are done so

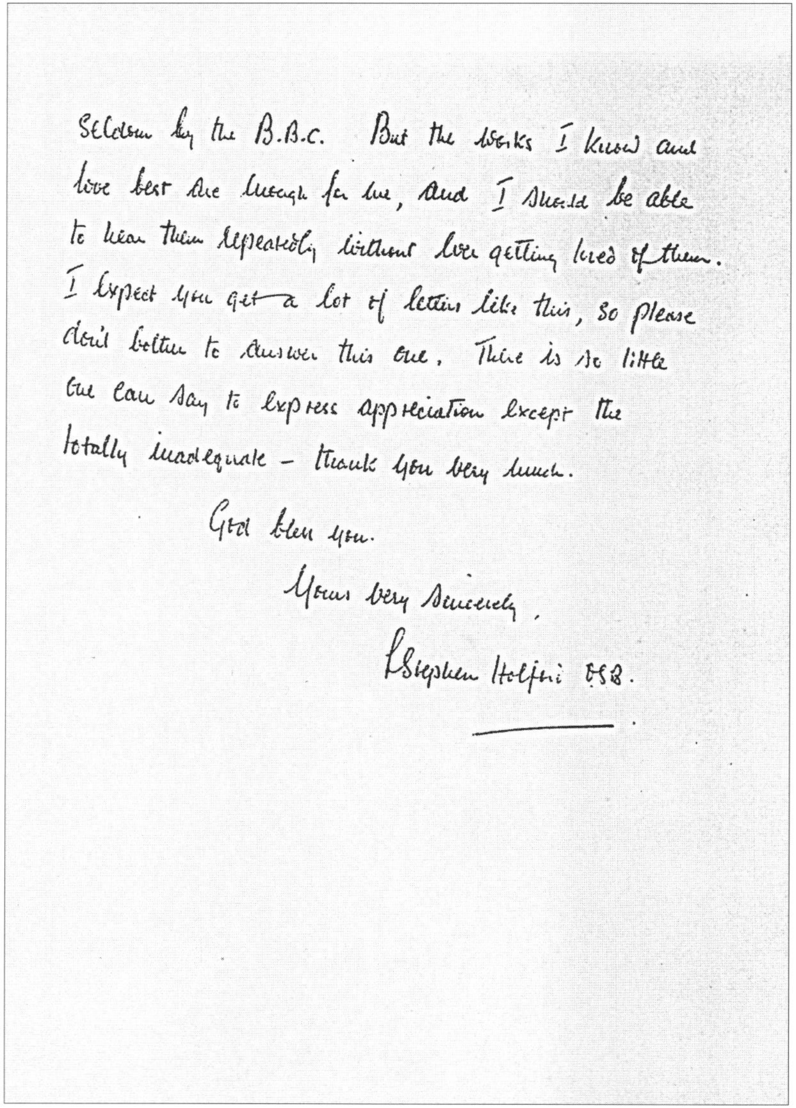

seldom by the B.B.C. But the works I know and love best are enough for me, and I should be able to hear them apparently without ever getting tired of them.

I expect you get a lot of letters like this, so please don't bother to answer this one. There is no little one can say to express appreciation except the totally inadequate — thank you very much.

God bless you.

Yours very sincerely,

[Stephen Hilfri] O.S.B.

One of the many dramatic moments in *Checkmate*.
(Photo, the Royal Opera House, Covent Garden)

have been tested if he had known, for example, the lengths to which the conductor of Foden's Motor Works Band – Fred Mortimer – and his son Harry, went when they discovered that Bliss's *Kenilworth* suite (mentioned above) was to be the test-piece for the 1936 National Brass Band Contest. They actually went to the trouble and expense of making a special visit to Kenilworth Castle to absorb its atmosphere, and of going to the cinema 'several times' to see *Things to Come* in order to be 'conversant with Bliss's musical style'.[1] One can imagine AB's amusement at reading this but, at the same time, his serious nod of approval at their professionalism.

'1937 was an exciting year for me,' wrote Bliss in his youthful and enthusiastic style, 'planning as I was my first ballet.'[2] He had been offered this opportunity by the Sadler's Wells Ballet Company (later to become The Royal Ballet) in preparation for their first ever appearance at the Théâtre des Champs Elysées in Paris; it was therefore an important and prestigious commission, a 'first' for him and for the Company.

He was not in the least over-awed by it. In fact, he already knew what dramatic subject the ballet was going to deal with: the game of chess. To many people, perhaps, chess appears a sedentary game and, to untutored observers, a dull one. But Bliss knew better; a life-long player himself, especially during his bachelor days in London with R.O. Morris, to whom the work is dedicated, he realised that the merciless logic of this game with its savage and brutal cut and thrust, interspersed with beguiling deceptions, could be transmuted by a skilled choreographer into a thrilling dramatic ballet, enhanced by brilliant designs for costumes and scenery, and music which fitted each mood perfectly. The war-like rumblings in Europe at the time no doubt had an effect on him:

Written at a time when the dramas of the chess game were terrifyingly echoed in the worsening European scene, 'Checkmate' has a power and a passionate expression that are still gripping in the theatre. The mood, surely set by the music of the Prologue, is one of inexorable tragedy; the bold melodic writing and the precisely stated atmosphere created by the dark orchestral colouring have an eloquence that sustains and embellishes the danced theme.[3]

The choreographer was Ninette de Valois, who had been directing at Sadler's Wells for six years, and the designer was McKnight Kauffer. But an important additional supporter, especially in the first and last stages, was Bridges Adams, one-time director of the Shakespeare Company at Stratford and an authority on all aspects of the theatre. He helped AB to work out the basic scenario and, just when the whole enterprise looked like foundering in Paris,

1. Harry Mortimer, *Harry Mortimer on Brass*, Alpha Books, Sherborne, Dorset 1981. p95 ff.
2. Bliss, op. cit p113.
3. *Musical Times*, Aug 1966, 'Bliss 75th Birthday no.' Clement Crisp, p674.

A portrait of Bliss in 1937, by 'Anthony'.

with a last-minute strike of the scene-shifters, he managed to take command and persuade them to set the stage just in time.[1] The conductor was Constant Lambert, Britain's most experienced ballet-conductor, whose own ballet – *Horoscope* – was written and produced in the same year as *Checkmate*. The cast included Frederick Ashton, Robert Helpmann, Michael Somes and Margot Fonteyn, so once again Bliss was fortunate to have such a star-studded list of artists to present his first work for the stage.

Checkmate was very well received and has, as the composer wrote, 'danced itself round a good part of the world since its first performance in Paris.'[2] But although 'it has been one of the most popular of English ballets on the Continent [it] has remained slightly outside the spirit of Sadler's Wells,' and it has been suggested that the reason for this is the startling modernity of the décor, 'a brilliant synthesis of modernisms – Cubism, Futurism, and the Syncretism of Kandinsky, all made more immediate for impact in the theatre.'[3] This may seem a strange reason for dropping a ballet out of a company's repertoire but luckily we still have the music regularly performed because Bliss made several concert suites from it, the one most usually heard being the 'Prologue and Five Dances' which comprise about half of the full score and are published by Novello.

A final word abut *Checkmate*:

It is, in effect, superb theatre; how much it owed to Bliss's experience in writing illustrative film music ... I dare not judge, but certainly part of the score's wonderful assurance must be due to the fact that Bliss was working on a scenario of which he was part author, and which he could adapt to suit his musical inspiration.[4]

After all the excitement in Paris, it was not very long before AB found himself abroad again, this time as a member of an international jury for the Ysaÿe Competition for Pianists in Brussels. It was the first experience he had had of this type of work and not one he wanted to repeat:

I have heard twenty-two pianists play the same piece by Bach, the same piece by Scarlatti, and expect to hear them sixty-three times more. Never again![5]

Nevertheless, he did do it again – for example, in Moscow, 1958, when the Chairman of the Jury was Emil Gilels, who had won twenty years earlier in Brussels. Nor was he put off the piano by hearing it played so much: in the following summer he accepted with alacrity an invitation from the British Council to compose a concerto for the instrument, to be performed by Solomon for

1. Bliss, op. cit. p115.
2. Bliss, op. cit. p115.
3. Kenneth Clarke, 'Ballet Décors', in *Gala Performance*, Collins 1955, p136.
4. *Musical Times*, op. cit.
5. Bliss, op. cit. p119.

Solomon at the piano, about 1939.

the British Week at the New York World's Fair. This composition turned out to be similar, in some respects, to the *Viola Sonata* for Tertis: the performer in each case was 'meticulous in making technical suggestions'[1] and in editing the concerto when it was completed in manuscript.

AB was again modest enough to find this type of collaboration 'stimulating', but whether it was in the end beneficial to the work is open to question. Spontaneity was an important element in his creativity and it is difficult to retain that in a work of art when you know that someone else – a future performer of the work, perhaps – is 'looking over your shoulder' (metaphorically speaking) ready to pounce on any detail which does not quite fit with his technique (imagine Richard Burbage prompting Shakespeare while he was writing Hamlet's soliloquies!). The *Concerto for Piano and Orchestra* is a big work, bold and confident in its form and style, with a hint of Liszt and Rachmaninoff in its design; but there are moments when a listener feels the constraint of the technician's hand descending on the music and longs for more of the freedom of the poet's imagination.

The concerto's first performance, with the New York Philharmonic Symphony Orchestra and Adrian Boult conducting, was at Carnegie Hall in June 1939. All the Bliss family were in New York for the great occasion and when the moment came for

1. Bliss, op. cit. p120.

Solomon to mount the platform AB found the eminent pianist in a nervous state saying he didn't feel he could go on and play; a kindly and gentle shove from the composer propelled him forwards and by the time he had perfectly executed the surging double octave passage of the piano entry all was well and the performance was acclaimed. The dedication of this work 'To the People of the United States of America' is an indication of the significance and importance Bliss and his sponsors attached to it; the music is extrovert and romantic, thus recalling AB's personal associations with the land of his father.

AB and Trudy were now determined to take a well-earned holiday with their two children in a part of America they had not previously seen, so after a short interval they packed up their camping gear and set out for Moosehead Lake, in Maine, about five hundred miles north of New York and conveniently *en route* for Montreal, from which port Bliss had booked passages back to England that Autumn. The two daughters – Barbara and Karen – were aged thirteen and seven, so the camping holiday in this remote beauty-spot was an ideal experience for them and a delightful break for their parents. But some vague news of the situation in Europe eventually reached them and they hurriedly returned to civilisation to discover what was happening. The awful truth then dawned: war had broken out, a passenger liner had already been sunk in the Atlantic, berths for civilians on other ships were extremely scarce; in any case there would be great risk in travelling to England now. When Bliss cabled Boult, who had already returned home, for his advice the answer he received was: wait where you are for the present. They waited, in an agony of suspense.

Albert Elkus, head of the music department at the university of California at Berkeley, had attended the performance of the piano concerto at Carnegie Hall and had asked AB, an old friend, if he would like to come as visiting professor the following January for a term or two, and Bliss had said he would consider it. Now the invitation seemed like a life-line. He accepted it and the die was cast, they would stay in America for the time being and await events; the period of doubt and indecision was over, for a while.

5 Recuperation

Olympian bards who sung
Divine ideas below,
Which always find us young,
And always keep us so.

From 'The Poet' – Ralph Waldo Emerson

The so-called 'phoney war' in Europe lasted for a year and during that time Bliss and his family lived a peaceful and pleasant life at Berkeley, close to the large University campus where he worked, giving a course of lectures on the history of British music from the fifteenth century to contemporary times. From the description of his methods in *As I Remember*, it is obvious that he brought to the lecture room the same imagination and enthusiasm which he bestowed on everything else he did. The students were lucky: he was a gifted teacher. The Blisses soon made close friends among colleagues of his in the Music Faculty but sometimes AB accepted conducting engagements outside the San Francisco area, for example in Los Angeles, and while there he visited Stravinsky and Schoenberg who were, fatefully, living in the same neighbourhood. He does not reveal much about the meeting with Stravinsky, who had only recently arrived in America and was very short of money, but the Schoenbergs gave him lunch and a gramophone recital of two of the host's string quartets which evidently moved them both to tears. Hospitality can induce unexpected emotions among great artists.

While on vacation in the summer of 1940, with Trudy's relations at Santa Barbara, AB set *Seven American Poems* which George Dannatt thought were 'probably, the best songs he wrote for voice and piano'.[1] The composer himself said that they expressed his sombre mood at that time and that 'each one … carries the burden of a vanished joy or beauty.'[2] He was beginning to feel once more the conflict of loyalties which had attacked him the previous year when he heard about the outbreak of war: whether to stay where he was with his wife and family, or to return to England where he might be needed; '… for weeks I hovered between one line of action and another.'[3] He had written to Adrian Boult at the BBC and to Bridges Adams at the British Council offering his services if they were required and now, in September, he heard from his brother Howard that the bombing of London had started; the

1. George Dannatt, op. cit. p17.   2. Bliss, op. cit. p126.   3. Bliss, op. cit p127.

'phoney war' had ended and this made his anxiety even worse. In America the mood was strongly pacifist; the country had recently emerged from recession and Franklin Roosevelt had been re-elected President on a programme of rehabilitation. He was confronted in Washington by men carrying bill-boards which said: 'KEEP OUT OF EUROPE: NO WAR!' and similar warnings. None of this can have been of any help to AB, whose strong sense of patriotism and duty had, rather ironically, been inherited from his American father. In the midst of this turmoil of perplexities, he received another letter from Bridges Adams listing all the reasons why he should stay where he was: he was over-age, he had served in one Great War with distinction, he had a duty to be with his family; above all, he must go on composing – this was his duty to mankind and to posterity.

Slightly mollified, and encouraged by Mrs Coolidge, he settled down sufficiently to compose a string quartet for the Pro Arte, an internationally famous ensemble who were based at this time in California. This work was published during the following year by Novello as *String Quartet No.1 in B flat*, although he had previously written two others which were withdrawn. The quartet is in the classical four-movement form (but with the slow movement coming third); there any resemblance to classical music ends, however, because the whole work is introspective in mood and about as different from a quartet by Haydn as it is possible to imagine. It has a great deal of tension, heightened by dissonant harmonies and sudden outbursts of loud music after periods of calm; it is also irresolute, as if the composer was searching for something (perhaps a solution to his problems at the time?) but, despite these qualifications, it is a delightful work; the parts for each instrument are beautifully blended and the second movement in particular ('Allegretto Grazioso') fulfils its title's claim to graciousness perfectly – it could only have been written by a master craftsman. This quartet is not for amateur performers; the notes are extremely difficult but most of all the 'tempo' for each different mood has to be exactly right. This matter of 'tempo' was one to which Bliss was exceptionally sensitive.

I have come to the conclusion that I do not so much mind wrong notes or a disregard of dynamics provided the basic tempo is right ... If my music is to make any impression it must move on, and not be static, that is the very essence of my own character ... A right pulse is for me the first essential factor in pleasurable listening.[1]

The reference here to 'movement' in relation to his own character is borne out by a recollection of one of AB's later friends who thinks that 'dash' is a word which suited him well, not only in the sense of 'moving on', but also in 'cutting a dash' – doing everything in style. 'He would certainly have been caught for speeding these days ...'[2]

1. Bliss, op. cit. p102.   2. Giles Easterbrook, with kind permission.

AB saying farewell to his students in the Music Department at Berkeley, April 1941.

In the light of this, it is easy to appreciate the extent of Bliss's impatience at not knowing whether he was needed in London and, if he was, how he was going to cross the Atlantic while it was infested with German submarines. There was nothing more he could do about it for the moment and that must have exasperated him even more. But a temporary diversion was the first performance of his quartet at Berkeley in April 1941, given by the Pro Arte, led on this occasion by Antonio Brosa whose interest in contemporary music as well as his brilliant playing ensured a sympathetic rendering. About a year later, the quartet was played for the first time in London, this time by the Griller Quartet, at one of the celebrated mid-day concerts at the National Gallery, timed to 'beat the Blitz' (ie to avoid the almost nightly bombing to which London was then being subjected).

It is no doubt a help for a lecturer on any artistic subject to have a work performed, a book published or a picture exhibited; students suddenly become aware that the person whose *obiter dicta* they have been digesting for so long can actually achieve something positive in the big wide world. AB's established reputation as a composer had preceded him at Berkeley but it was probably enhanced by the performance of his quartet and there is no doubt about the warmth of his students' feelings when he said farewell to them shortly after it had taken place (see illustration). He had received a letter from Kenneth Wright, Director of Overseas Music at the BBC, asking him if he would be willing to come to help him in his department. This was the signal he had been half-hoping for and half-dreading; but at least he was now able to make a decision and in this he was marvellously supported by Trudy:

My wife remained always wonderfully understanding, never trying to influence me one way or another; she knew with the clearest intuition what was involved, and what might be the consequence in future happiness of the final decision ... she came to New York to see me set off for Canada; it was the most anguished moment through which I have lived.[1]

The anguish for Trudy was just as great and for their daughters (aged 14 and 9 at the time) she had to bear the suffering too. Barbara, the elder, remembers the tension they all endured before the decision to part was finally made but she has no doubt at all that he *had* to return to England because 'it was his duty and duty meant a great deal to him, although he never made a show of it.'[2]

When he arrived at Montreal there was a long delay while the large convoy was assembled, and the voyage across the treacherous ocean took three weeks; a route to the north had to be taken in the hope of avoiding one of the enemy warships hunting just such a convoy as this, so it was the end of June, 1941, when they finally reached Avonmouth. Bliss had sent a stream of letters to Trudy and the two girls, some of which he included with 'some

1. Bliss, op. cit. p127 & 130.
2. Mrs R. Gatehouse (née Barbara Bliss), with kind permission.

The building the bombs destroyed on 10 May 1941 – the interior of the Queen's Hall, London.

qualms', as he said, in the autobiography.[1] Perhaps the note which he handed to Trudy in a sealed envelope on their parting in new York is the most intimate and the one which best expresses his emotional state:

Dearest love – Patience and Courage to us both. What we have between us is indestructible – so I defy anybody or anything to break it.

I shall write a long letter air mail immediately on arrival in Toronto I carry you and the 2 darlings with me.

A.[2]

What he found when he reached London was a city changed beyond recognition, especially in the hours between dusk and dawn when every light was blacked out; some of the favourite old land-marks had already been reduced to rubble (the Queen's Hall, scene of so many memorable concerts for Bliss, had been destroyed in a raid the previous month). 'I felt I had wandered into some black nightmare,'[3] he recalled. But the feeling lightened quickly when he got in touch again with friends and acquaintances, of whom he had a wide circle. Among the closest were Maurice and Nancy Farquharson, neighbours at Hampstead before the AB's left for America. Arthur and Maurice had been together in the Guards towards the end of World War I; later, Maurice Farquharson joined the staff of the BBC and became Secretary, so he and AB shared another interest. An invitation to stay with them came before he left America:

1. Bliss, op. cit p130.
2. Ibid, p131.
3. Bliss, op. cit. p139.

In 1941 we heard that AB was anxious to come back – the family had given up their house here and gone to America ... so we wired to him suggesting that he came to stay with us *for a fortnight* whilst he looked for somewhere to live – he came, and stayed for two years![1]

They obviously got on famously. AB had named them 'M'ong and N'ang' after visiting the Chinese Exhibition in London with them and Trudy in the early 1930s, and he simply carried on in 1941 where he had left off – and with such a friendly couple, why not? They were willing to pander to his every eccentricity:

Arthur had a very lively personality – he was often extremely witty and tended to be at his very best at breakfast. This was not *our* best time as we either wanted to read the papers or ponder the day ahead ... however, he was equally lively sometimes at the end of the day ... We had just returned one evening from the theatre – by Tube – A. decided that one way was shorter than another and he would demonstrate his point, so we parted company and he went one way and we the other. There was very little in it but we arrived home to find A. standing at the top of the stairs in his pyjamas, yawning. He had obviously run the whole way ...[2]

But Bliss had come back to England to do a job of work, not for fun and games, and it was not long before his ambition prompted him to suggest to Boult that he (AB) took over the post of Director of Music at the BBC while Boult concentrated on conducting the orchestra.[3] Even more boldly, he sent a statement of 'Music Policy' to the Director General, setting out his ideas for the re-organization of broadcast music; its most far-seeing suggestion (which he headed 'A Fantasy') was that there should be three channels – one for what he called 'great' music, one for relaxation and the third for popular entertainment.[4] This dream eventually came true but not until later.

Meanwhile, he continued to renew old friendships and to describe some of them to Trudy in long letters, including this version of his sojourn with the Farquharsons:

... I can't tell you how deeply grateful I am to Nancy and Peggy[5] – Nancy will not have me live anywhere else in London at any price. I have tried, because I can't believe you always want a guest in your house – but she just gets in a rage and says 'no!' ... She and Maurice *very* pleased with your gifts and message ... The seasons in England are really most magical, and I look forward to a *whole year* sometime with you in Pen Pits – see how I have changed! – but the emphasis is as always on the words – *with you.*[6]

These letters to his family in America are liberally quoted in *As I Remember* and they reveal more about AB's personality and

1. Mrs Nancy Farquharson, with kind permission.
2. Mrs Nancy Farquharson, ibid.
3. This in fact took place early the following year.
4. Bliss, op. cit pp149-152.
5. Nancy Farquharson's sister.
6. Op. cit. pp147-8.

A flying boat moored in Poole Harbour during the war. This BOAC Speedbird, named 'Salisbury', may have brought Trudy and her daughters back to England in 1943.

By permission of Mr Peter Rose, son of Captain 'Tommy' Rose, the pilot.

his feelings at this time than any other passages in the book. There is space however to include only a few snippets:

A touch of gentle wit: '... I welcome this night of fire-watching because I get a chance of writing to you ...'[1]

An occasional confession: 'What a lucky man I am!' (referring to the reservoir of beauty and love his family provide).[2]

Concern (to Trudy) about Japan's attack in Pearl harbour: 'Is this going to prolong the war and our separation?'[3]

Paternal and sentimental (to each daughter): 'You are a good daughter to write to me so often and I always get a thrill when I see the handwriting on my desk.'[4]

In April 1942, he was able to go down and have a look at Pen Pits. Memories and hopes engulfed him: '... how lovely it all looked there ... I felt somehow that before very long we shall all be happily playing about there.'[5]

Finally, to Trudy: 'It is nearly a year now – it will never come again – how glad I am! perhaps this next year will bring peace & you & happiness ...'[6]

1. Bliss, op. cit. p145.
2. Ibid. p144.
3. Ibid. p146
4. Ibid. op. cit. pp.153, 156.
5. Ibid. p152.
6. Ibid. p155.

The next year, 1943, did not bring peace but it did bring Trudy and her daughters. Intrepid and indomitable, she determined to make the hazardous voyage back to England and eventually obtained all the necessary permits to sail in a Portuguese ship from Philadelphia to Lisbon, and thence by flying boat to Poole, where they landed on 5 November. 'That evening', Bliss wrote, abruptly, 'I dived into the black obscurity of Waterloo Station – and found them.'[1] It was the end of the longest separation he and Trudy had in their fifty years of marriage. On the published score of his next big composition (*Miracle in the Gorbals* – see below) the dedication is: 'To Trudy, Barbara, Karen – thanksgiving for November 5th, 1943.'

They lived for a time in a flat in Cavendish Square and it was not very long before they were able to re-open the retreat in Somerset and it was while they were there that a young girl, aged about nine, often stayed with them and became known as their 'Little Pin-Up'. She returned the compliment by writing to him as 'Dear Micetroe'. Julia Harland, as she was then, was the daughter of Peter Harland, FRIBA, the architect of Pen Pits, and she was sent to a boarding school near Wincanton (her parents were living in London) so that she could escape from the bombing and have a home – Pen Pits – to go to at half-terms. On these occasions, AB began by collecting her from the school, but soon asked her to wait for him at the gate at the bottom of the drive. She had noticed that the Headmistress was always hovering to buttonhole AB when he collected or delivered her, anxious to be seen talking to an important visitor, so she asked him if that was the reason for the change of plan. 'Yes,' he replied, 'I don't know how you survive such a gorgon, she makes me feel like a school boy again. Not good for me!'[2]

Croquet foursome at Pen Pits: Peter Harland (back), his daughter Julia (left), his wife Liza and AB.

1. Ibid. p164.
2. This and the following recollections – Mrs J. Wadell (née Harland) with kind permission.

AB's music room at Pen Pits.

At Pen Pits, Julia used to go and watch him stealthily through the window of his 'den', a short distance from the house, where he composed:

I would stand on tip-toe and be spellbound watching the notes he was writing just fly across the manuscript pages. The clefs and notes were executed so beautifully and quickly, I had never seen anyone write so fast before, let alone compose a music score. He would then get up and try a passage on the piano but he wrote for long stretches ... I would long for a game of croquet which happened the moment he got stuck. He would come out and say, 'Time for a quick game', letting me have the first shot (which was usually the only turn I had), then he would whiz round happily and say, 'I've finished now, you practise,' and dive back to his music-room for more work.

The little girl relished the comfortable and peaceful atmosphere of the house, a real haven compared with school, 'another world' as she recalls it, and she writes now:

I realise how disciplined and organized they both were. Trudy, being American, brought the new world with her which made their life-style seem very modern and exciting. They were a remarkable couple; he with his boundless energy and vitality, she with her love of nature and outdoor life. How lucky I was to have been a young guest of 'dear Micetroe's!

After the return of his family, AB stayed on as Director of Music at the BBC for a few months but then resigned and returned to full-time composition. His work for the Corporation did not go unrecognized and a modern historian has recorded that:

It was Bliss, therefore, who was formally responsible for the still further extended musical output of 1943 and early 1944 ... Particular emphasis was placed during this year on British works ...

72

adding in a footnote that,

In October 1943 Bliss wrote to the 'Sunday Times' that during the course of the year 27% of the music broadcast had been British, of which 17% was by contemporaries. The governors had decided in 1942 ... that while the primary consideration in music policy should be quality, 'when the merits were equal as between enemy and British composers, preference should be given to the British'[1]

When Harry Mortimer was applying in 1942 for the BBC post of Brass and Military Bands Supervisor he was told that if he was offered the job he would have to give up his Band work. Dismayed, he consulted the 'always sympathetic Arthur Bliss', who agreed that this was as ridiculous as asking Moiseivitsch to be 'head of Piano Recitals' provided he gave up playing the piano.[2] It was this kind of internal problem which AB found very tiresome at the BBC; these matters seemed petty to him, yet he recognized their crucial importance to the individuals concerned. It must have been a relief to leave them behind and to be his own boss again. However, the family link with the Corporation was not immediately broken because after her return home Trudy did some radio broadcasting, first on 'The Kitchen Front', then on the North American Overseas Service which she continued for a number of years. She also wrote *Memorial Concert*, a play for radio, which was broadcast on the Home Service in March 1946, and for which Bliss composed the music; the BBC Symphony Orchestra played it, conducted by Lionel Salter, with Max Rostal (solo violin).

Apart from this, Bliss had composed nothing since his return to England except a ballet-score for Robert Helpmann and Michael Bentall, *Miracle in The Gorbals*. This score, transcribed by Bliss as a concert suite published by Novello in 1945, was praised at the time of its Sadler's Wells performances during the last year of the war, and when it was reviewed retrospectively later:

For a number of reasons this must rank as one of the outstanding creations of contemporary ballet. It dares more than other works; its success is all the greater. The story is the popular one of the return of the Saviour to the modern scene. It is obviously dramatic, but presents many dangers from offensive bad taste to mawkishness. It is a tribute to the success of the ballet that the highest praise has come from the religious press. The setting for this visitation is the Gorbals in Glasgow. This is a singularly happy choice, enabling the choreographer to probe behind the Palais de Danse atmosphere of the crowded city slum on a Saturday night and to find the true emotional depths of these people in their national Scottish dances. Arthur Bliss has written a brilliant score on those lines, making full use of natural sounds, such as the wailing of a ship's siren, and also of Scottish national music. The result is not a sordid slum picture, but a sympathetic study that presents people as they really are, that looks under the surface and can rise to lyrical heights.

1. Asa Briggs, *The History of Broadcasting in the UK* Vol III, 1979, p583.
2. H. Mortimer, op. cit. passim.

One of the most moving moments in the whole of ballet occurs when the stranger brings the young suicide to life. At first she still belongs to the world of the spirit, then, gradually, as the blood warms within her, she breaks into some country dance remembered from childhood. The person who opposes and finally brings about the death of the stranger is no mere villain but a complex personality, capable of great good as well as evil. For the first time this is characterization in the round; these are not puppets but living people. There are two directions that Helpmann might have taken but has not: the impression of a big city, already brilliantly done by Jooss, or the presentation of a social problem, also within the province of Jooss. What he has done is to say, 'Here is a mass of people in a sordid slum. They all look more or less the same. How do they react both as individuals and as a group in a particular emergency?' The Ballet is a working out of that, done with great directness but with a subtlety that gradually reveals itself. These tough dwellers in the dockland slum are suddenly moved by the primitive fear of a mountain people when confronted with death.

In this modern miracle play Helpmann, Bliss, and the painter Burra have introduced something new to ballet.[1]

In February 1946, The Royal Opera House, Covent Garden, which had been closed for much of the war, re-opened with *The Sleeping Beauty*, produced by the Sadler's Wells Ballet Company. This was a triumph for British ballet because the Company became established as the favourite with London audiences and thus restricted foreign companies to a visiting role. In April of the same year, Bliss's *Adam Zero* was the first new ballet to be produced at Covent Garden for some years; it was another Helpmann/ Bentall production and Bliss always considered it his best ballet-score. He dedicated it to Constant Lambert, the work's first conductor. But in spite of such an auspicious launch, this ballet did not remain in the repertoire – to Bliss's regret – and the reason usually given is that the choreography depended too much on mime (Helpmann's great strength) and not sufficiently on classical dance, which had distinguished *Checkmate*. One writer called it 'a mammoth conglomeration of stage tricks not even made bearable by the choreographer's own superb acting as the protagonist'[2] an unfortunate verdict for Bliss whose music subsequently stood little chance of survival except in the piano solo arrangement he made for Novello in 1948.[3]

These two ballet-scores (*Miracle* and *Adam*) were both written mainly in the 'den' at Pen Pits, no doubt observed by Julia, but another secret whose existence she might have discovered, if she had understood its significance was a new folder, which could have been headed 'JBP – Opera', for it was at about this time – the summer of 1945 – that AB began his correspondence with Priestley concerning the operatic work – later called *The Olympians* – which occupied him exclusively for almost three years.

1. Arnold Haskell, *Ballet*, Pelican 1955, pp173–4.
2. Clive Barnes, *Ballet in Britain since the War*, Thrift Books, 1953, p27.
3. S. Craggs, op. cit. pp45–46.

A scene from Act II of *The Olympians*. (Courtesy of the Royal Opera House, Covent Garden)

A good deal has been written about English opera during the last few decades, but not very much literature on the national product was available before about the middle of the century, perhaps because there was little to write about. English composers of 'grand' opera (that is, a work – all sung – on a large scale, about a serious subject) were scarce, apart from several by Stanford, and one by Sullivan. But a writer who did attempt, with success, to describe the contemporary state of English opera was Edward Dent, Bliss's mentor at Cambridge and by 1940, when he wrote his short book, *Opera*, he was the acknowledged authority on the subject. Being a linguist as well as a musician, he attempted to explain clearly why British audiences on the whole prefer dramatic and heroic roles to be sung in any language but their own. He also addressed one of the main problems of writing an operatic score to English words: '… how to manage the plain statements about commonplace things which are unavoidable in order to keep the drama going,' concluding that 'Much depends on whether the words declaimed are metrical or not, and whether one can conveniently beat time to their musical setting.'[1]

75

Priestley, and of course Bliss, took immense trouble to compose words, and then music, which moved the dramatic action along smoothly; the fact that they were able to do so without serious disagreements does them both great credit. But the length of time it took to complete the work – nearly three years – gives an indication of the difficulties they encountered, in placing our language in a musical setting; at one point in their lengthy correspondence, Priestley actually suggested that in a certain passage it might be better if Bliss wrote the music first and he added the words to it.[2]

The plot was based on a legend that after the gods of Olympus had ceased to be worshipped on earth, some of them became free-lance actors touring Europe to find work year after year; but once in every century, on Midsummer Night, they miraculously became gods again with all their old powers restored. This fantasy took place, for the purposes of the opera, in a small town in the south of France in the mid-summer of 1836. Half the characters were therefore human – the landlady of an inn, the local Curé, a landowner, his daughter and her suitor, a young poet – while the other half were gods and goddesses in disguise – Jupiter, Venus, Diana, Bacchus, Mars and Mercury. In the first act the problems of the humans are exposed (the landowner wanting his daughter to marry someone else, the landlady owing money, the actors unable to pay their bill – and so on), in the second the gods become gods again and have a rousing time playing the dickens with the human situation, and in the third everything is settled satisfactorily and the gods go back to their hack-acting. It is a plot with obvious dramatic potential and anyone who has read a Priestley novel or seen one of his plays will be able to imagine how he revelled in manipulating the various human and incorporeal predicaments.

This story does not sound quite like those usually encountered in grand opera and indeed it was not; it was a semi-comic romantic fantasy, and perhaps it would have been more appropriately staged at Sadler's Wells instead of Covent Garden. Bliss was inspired to write some fine music, especially for the concerted items with a large chorus and an orchestra of at least seventy-five players, but whether such grand resources were really ideal for the scale and weight of the piece is an open question. Professor Dent thought they were not. After seeing the opera three times (and enjoying it more on each occasion), he wrote Bliss a very warm letter of congratulation but included these reservations:

The real trouble about the opera is that like Mozart, Busoni and others, you have put everything you had into it, and there is too much stuff – it makes the opera feel very long and rather exhausting though never tedious. I think it is all much too 'grand' and I should have preferred it treated more as opéra comique ... your choruses are all on the long side,

1. E.J. Dent, *Opera*, Pelican Books 1945, p91.
2. Bliss, op. cit. p177.

and very much on the massive side ... when I read the libretto I felt I wanted to set them in much livelier rhythms and lighter in texture.[1]

There are two quite short passages in the last act which prove Dent's point: first, a little classical minuet for the daughter and the poet and then, shortly afterwards, a jaunty jig for the father, with a jazzy rhythm; in both of these passages the scoring is light and the effect of heavy 'grand' opera is lifted.

The resources of Covent Garden in 1949 (the first performance was on 27 September) may have been large but they were unfortunately inefficient. First, a clash of temperament between the conductor and producer meant they did not communicate at all during later rehearsals; secondly, one of the principals failed to turn up until ten days before the first night; and thirdly, at the final dress rehearsal which the press attended, the third act was a disaster and the designer was nowhere to be found when difficulties with the scenery occurred. No wonder the composer retired to his club for most of the first performance, perhaps to console himself with the *Memoirs* of Berlioz, or something even more stimulating. He would not have been too pleased to discover that the programme on that first night described his work as an 'Opera in Three Acts by J.B. Priestley. Music by Arthur Bliss'.

There was a revival of the opera in a concert performance at the Royal Festival Hall in 1971, to celebrate AB's eightieth birthday, which prompted a number of critics to regret that he had not been encouraged to compose more for the opera house; to listen now to a recording of a concert performance while following a score – even a piano score – is to marvel at the inventiveness and often the sheer beauty of the music. However, the failure of the 1949 production was a disappointment which AB was able to put behind him, as he was able to do with any personal reverse, and it was not long before he and Priestley were discussing a plot for another opera. This ability to pick himself up from a knock-down blow, grit his teeth and begin again was one of the most admirable sides of his character; in the words of Sir Charles Groves during his very moving tribute to Bliss, broadcast by the BBC on the evening of his death, '... his mind and heart were always looking forward.'

His commitment to British music and musicians, the encouragement he gave to amateur performers – especially to the young – and his growing reputation as a leading composer of his generation were now crowned (June 1950) with the honour of a knighthood in the Birthday Honours of that year. This timely recognition coincided happily with the celebration of his silver wedding. But it was not like AB to be tempted to sit back and rest on his laurels at this high point in his career; he was soon hard at work again at his desk.

1. Quoted in Bliss, op. cit. p181–2.

As so often happened when he had just completed a dramatic

Bliss and Priestley discussing another opera at the latter's house on the Isle of Wight, 1950.

work, he now turned to 'pure' or 'absolute' music for his next composition, another string quartet. This was written for (although not dedicated to) the Griller Quartet, old friends of the composer, who first performed it at the Edinburgh Festival of that year. Ten years separated this work from its predecessor in that mode and the two quartets are very different: the earlier one, it may be remembered, was composed in America when AB was perplexed about whether to return to war-time England, but this one was the product of a happy and triumphant period in his family life (his elder daughter, Barbara, had married Richard Gatehouse two years previously) and this change in fortune and circumstances shows in the music, which is full of confidence and dash. The slow movement ('Sostenuto'), which comes second in order, is described by Bliss as revealing a new facet of his 'musical personality'[1] and by this he may have been referring to a departure from his previous tendency to roam when writing sustained passages for strings. In this five-minute section for mostly muted instruments, the steps are meditative but deliberate; the music knows where it wants to go, taking its cue from the first bar of a unison note followed by a tooth-drilling discord – definitely not music to induce slumber. The following movement, a 'Scherzo', is equally purposeful but in a totally different manner – all leaps and bounds and sizzling flights of virtuosity; again, it is not a

1. Bliss, op. cit. p186.

work for amateurs, alas! In fact, very little of AB's instrumental music is suitable for amateur performers; he was a professional composer, writing for professionals. This quartet was his last chamber music work and over twenty years later he told his friend, George Dannatt, that he thought it was his best work, adding, a moment later, 'My best work in chamber music, I mean.'[1]

With regard to AB's professionalism, this is a good moment to record his work for the Performing Right Society, of which he was elected vice-chairman in this year (1950) and president four years later, a post which he held until his death. It was the first time the Society had a composer in charge rather than a publisher.[2] It certainly needed a steady, forward-looking controller during the 1950s and '60s: after the boom years of the war ('Music While you Work' and canned music incessantly broadcast) there was a period when the Society failed to keep its income from dues abreast of inflation and performances, especially following the huge increase in broadcast music. Very often it was forced to go to the courts in order to raise sufficient funds to pay royalties and 'For those without alternative sources of income the Society could do very little.'[3] Some composers and performers of popular music, mainly from America, were making large fortunes in this country, while some others, mainly British, were impoverished.

All this changed when the Beatles arrived on the scene (John Lennon and Paul McCartney joined the PRS in 1962)[4] but even then the General Council of the Society, at which AB usually presided, had long meetings to discuss what could be done for those who were excluded from this prosperity. Michael Freegard who joined the staff at about that time and became Secretary and later General Manager remembers AB's 'great interest in young composers and other musicians and how forward-looking he was, often speculating about how things were going to develop in the future long after his own life time.'[5] He also recalls the occasion in 1966 when AB led the PRS delegation to the biennial Congress of the International Confederation of Societies of Authors and Composers (of which he was also President!) in Prague. All the meetings of this organization were conducted in French, in which AB was not fluent, so '... the meetings were chaired by the Vice-President ... and Sir Arthur sat patiently alongside him in his shirt-sleeves and braces (it was very hot) for many hours. I remember thinking how very Blimpish he looked and how misleading an impression this gave – I had already discovered what a lively mind he had and how knowledgeable he was on many subjects besides music.'[6]

Mr Freegard recalls that at this congress in Prague, because of

1. George Dannatt, Notes for Hyperion CD recording of Bliss's String Quartets, 1985 with kind permission.
2. The History of the PRS, from its inception in 1914, is contained in *Harmonious Alliance* by Cyril Ehrlich, OUP 1989.
3. Op.Cit. p101.
4. C. Ehrlich, Ibid.
5. M. Freegard, with kind permission.
6. Ibid.

economic circumstances, it had been decided that only Trudy Bliss and Ethel Boosey could accompany the British PRS delegation but:

Conditions in Prague were not comfortable and morale among the spouseless other delegates was low ... so Trudy played a big part in rallying everyone's spirits and keeping us cheerful, among other things organizing a boating trip on the River Vltava. They were both so much liked and admired by everyone in that international circle, as indeed by everyone fortunate enough to come into contact with them, myself included.[1]

The PRS Presidency involved Bliss in many other meetings abroad – for example, conferences on copy-right protection in practically every capital in Europe – and it may seem strange that a hard-working and sensitive musician such as he could willingly undertake these arduous journeys in order to sit for hours in some gloomy apartment while a succession of pompous lawyers boomed out their boring speeches through loudspeakers in a foreign language. He said he did it as a kind of relaxation from composition: 'In the lulls between the times when music takes hold of me, and temporarily I lie becalmed, I find it necessary to occupy myself with alternative activities.'[2] Another reason he gave was that he had inherited from his father '... the need to do some practical administrative work, to organise and plan, to see theories put into practice.'[3] but one suspects that the overriding reason, which he did not want to publicize, was to give some practical help to artists less fortunate than himself: why, otherwise, would so many people – some of them eminent musicians like himself, others just musical appreciators – have emphasized this benevolent quality in his character in their tributes on his birthdays and finally in their obituaries?

You, Arthur, have given us 50 years of active responsibility. Few of our juniors have not been helped directly or indirectly by your practical benevolence.[4]

1. M. Freegard, Ibid.
2. Bliss, op. cit p186.
3. Ibid.
4. Part of a letter to AB on his 75th Birthday from Benjamin Britten, dated 4.8.66. Quoted in *As I Remember*, 1989 ed. p292.

6 Master of the Music

But if it is a sin to covet honour
I am the most offending soul alive

Shakespeare – from King Henry V,
Act IV, Scene II

Kathleen Ferrier proclaimed herself and her glorious voice to the musical public when she began recording for Columbia towards the end of the war, and her dramatic powers were revealed when she appeared in Britten's new opera, *The Rape of Lucretia*, at Glyndebourne in 1946. From then and for the next five years, she undertook a punishing schedule of engagements all over Britain and abroad. Her natural charm of personality won the hearts of all who met her and the honest refinement of her musicianship captured the enthusiasm of the leading international conductors of the day, including Barbirolli, Boult, Sargent and Bruno Walter. Soon the major contralto/mezzo-soprano parts in oratorio, opera and lieder were all hers for the taking and she took these engagements with incredulous delight and apparent disregard for the cumulative effect they might have on her health. London, Edinburgh, Glyndebourne, New York, Ottawa, Chicago, Amsterdam, Utrecht, Copenhagen ... the list of her conquests was endless and so were the demands on her stamina: 'From Carlisle to Covent Garden in five years!' she exclaimed, 'Lucky Kath!'[1]

But fortune did not bestow her favours without impediments: Kathleen's private and domestic life was seriously hampered by the demands of her career and although she revelled in the new experiences of lavish praise and luxurious living, she secretly longed for a husband and family, peace and contentment.[2] But most of all, and of overriding significance, she worried about her health and it was in March 1951 that she had to have an operation for cancer of the breast. She recovered and during the summer, in spite of weekly visits to hospital, managed to fulfil all her engagements, including some in Holland, London and Edinburgh. When she finally returned home to rest in the autumn, Bliss brought her a new work he had written specially for her, a 'scena' (an extended piece for solo singer and orchestra) which he called *The Enchantress*. The words had been arranged by a poet-friend of his – Henry Reed – from one of the 'Idylls' of

---

1. Winifred Ferrier, *Kathleen Ferrier, Her Life.* Penguin Books 1959, p97.
2. Ibid. Passim.

The bronze bust of Sir Arthur Bliss by Maurice Lambert, 1951, now in the Music Department of Cambridge University Library.

Theocritus, concerning a proud lady from Syracuse, Simaetha, who, deserted by her lover, resorted to witchcraft to entice him back to her arms. AB realised at once, when he met Kathleen at her house, that it would be difficult to imagine a character less appropriate for her to represent. He admitted as much to her but 'she only laughed – and went on singing gloriously'.[1] The music is intensely dramatic, as it had to be, and in the middle section – when Simaetha asks for the heart of her lover to be melted – there is some of Bliss's most delightful lyricism, but it is not a work which suited the character (or the state of health) of its dedicatee.

Kathleen Ferrier broadcast *The Enchantress* from Manchester with the BBC Northern Orchestra, conducted by Groves, in October, just two years before she died. In their short acquaintance, Bliss had been immensely moved, as were so many others, by her artistic integrity: 'Our encounter was brief, but to me unforgettable', he wrote.[2]

There were other memorable events and commissions awaiting him during the next few years. In 1951 the Royal Festival Hall was opened, part of the Festival of Britain to mark the centenary of the Great Exhibition. This was the first big event signifying a departure from the years of drab austerity which followed the end of the war, but for musical people everywhere it was of even greater consequence because it provided a replacement for the much loved Queen's Hall. The new concert hall was also to be the venue for important occasions in Arthur Bliss's life: a number of his works received first performances there and he was to be honoured there several times, one of the earliest being a Royal Philharmonic Society concert of his music in January 1955, so the RFH must have won a place in his affection.

On one occasion when he was on duty to meet the Queen who was attending a concert there, it had been arranged that her Majesty would arrive at a side entrance and there was quite a long walk before they reached the staircase leading to the Royal Box. It happened that their route led the party through two lines of book-stalls and this gave AB an opportunity for a conversational topic; noticing a book with a picture of a horse's head on the front cover, he picked it up and said, 'This might interest Your Majesty, perhaps?' 'Oh, yes,' the Queen replied, taking the book and turning a few pages. 'You know, I don't think I have this one.' Congratulating himself on a lucky choice, AB summoned an assistant who at once begged Her Majesty to accept the book as a gift, which she graciously did and, very obviously pleased, said to AB laughingly: 'It's nice to get something for nothing occasionally, don't you agree Sir Arthur?' The humorous significance of her remark only struck him fully as they mounted the stairs when he suddenly exploded with laughter, causing slight consternation among the party.[3]

1. Bliss, op. cit. p191.
2. Bliss, op. cit. p192.
3. As told to Mrs Richard Gatehouse by Bliss, with kind permission.

Queen Elizabeth the Queen Mother at the Coronation of her daughter.

However, his first official musical assignment with the young Queen Elizabeth was a request to write a piece for her Coronation Service in Westminster Abbey. This was *Processional*, for organ and orchestra, which was played for the entrance of Queen Elizabeth the Queen Mother. AB and Trudy both attended this great event, 'By Command of the Queen', and he received the Coronation Medal.[1]

Earlier, in 1952, he had composed a piano sonata for Noel Mewton-Wood, a young pianist of great promise who had already performed Bliss's Concerto for the instrument with success. The Sonata was broadcast by the BBC in April of the following year and it caused AB great sadness when he heard the news of Mewton-Wood's suicide two years later.

It was at about this time that he and Trudy decided, with great regret, to sell Pen Pits. His increasing work and the difficulty of getting away for week-ends (in those days it took three hours or more to get down from London to Somerset by train or car) made it too much of a liability, but they retained a fond affection for the place and its beauty, re-visiting it several times after the sale and being delighted to see how well it, and the garden, were preserved. As AB recalled later: 'Only the secluded little music-room, in which I wrote so much, has taken on a wan, ghost like and rather sad appearance.'[2]

The Blisses now moved to a larger London house – 8, The Lane, St John's Wood – and it was here that AB composed most of the music which completed his total output. He very much liked the new house and enjoyed composing there, which was just as well because his commissions during 1953 included a violin concerto for the BBC (with Campoli named as the soloist), a new musical edition of *The Beggar's Opera* for a film and a major work for the

1. S. Craggs, op. cit. p32.   2. Bliss, op. cit. p193.

City of Birmingham Orchestra. He makes only one very brief mention of *The Beggar's Opera* in *As I Remember* but it was an important commission – the film was produced by Laurence Olivier and Herbert Wilcox and directed by Peter Brook – and it must have occupied him for many hours (AB's concert version contains thirty-five items).[1] However he admits to 'taking his time' over the violin concerto and, as always, he makes generous acknowledgement of his debt to the first performer, Campoli, whose advice he sought and obtained throughout. But the music is unmistakably Bliss, with its bold statements, contrasted moods and uncompromising difficulties; the only section of it in which Campoli himself can be clearly identified is in the last movement, a zingaro-style dance, which was invented as a compliment to the technique of the soloist. The first performance took place in the Festival Hall in May 1955, and the critical reaction was encouraging, if predictable:

It was time that Sir Arthur Bliss wrote such a work, for *bravura* and *cantilena* are much in his line; and it is sixteen years since he gave us a concerto ... it abounds in brilliant passages and lyrical melody, in generous solo sonority and exhilarating *leggiero* effects ... The ideas are purposeful and fertile; all are not immediately striking but they are entirely characteristic, and apt to their context ... As we may expect, Bliss finds beguiling and individual orchestral colours to support the violin; the rhythms are typically invigorating ... it contains much that is strong and grateful ... Mr. Campoli gave a dazzling and warmly mellifluous account of the solo part.[2]

Not that Bliss took a great deal of notice of critical reactions, for once a work was completed he was anxious only to go forward to the next one and to adapt himself to its particular demands, as another writer shrewdly observed:

Whether we like his music or not is a matter of indifference to him or at any rate to the artist in him. He says categorically what he has to say, and there is an end to it. Really an end, once he has finished a work, for he will make the next one an entirely different task. He likes setting new problems for himself over and over again and then solving them by finding a new style suited to them. This does not mean that he is inconsistent; indeed he has progressed, from almost freakishly enterprising though never tentative beginnings, with remarkable single-mindedness. Not all his works appeal to any one hearer. Some have been repellent, some almost enchantingly attractive; but each one has been, whether a work of art or only an *object d'art*, shaped with unfailing skill and determination.[3]

'Skill and determination' were the corner-stones of AB's life in music. They provided a platform on which he exercised all the panache (a favourite word of his) which his zest for life gave him.

1. Craggs, op. cit. p68.
2. *The Times*, 12.5.55.
3. Eric Blom, *Music in England*, Pelican Books, revised edn. 1947, p267.

'Master of the Queen's Musick': Sir Arthur at his piano in 1953.

This quality is generally a characteristic associated with young composers, and he certainly demonstrated it in his youth, but the extraordinary fact about Arthur Bliss's musical career is that he continued to show it through middle-age and almost to the end of his life. It is remarked upon by many people who knew him well: he always impressed them with his champagne-like attitude to life, cloaked under an outward calm:

He has an attractive wit and a twinkle in the eye that preclude formality of any kind and make him ... the most delightful of companions. His natural instinct, critical though he can be, is to praise rather than to find fault: and he has a sense of charity all too rare in artistic circles. Bliss, in the midst of a crisis at rehearsals in theatre or concert hall, is always the calmest person present; but, if the occasion calls for it, this ex-Guardsman can be a hard hitter.[1]

This was written shortly before AB's sixty-second birthday and only a few months before he received that most stately accolade of the musical establishment, the Mastership of the Queen's Musick. The 'k' is an anachronism dating back to the time of Charles I who founded the office in 1625 and Bliss favoured its use. In the seventeenth and eighteenth centuries the main duty of the Masters was to set to music Odes celebrating, in flowery language, occasions like Royal Birthdays, peace treaties, the safe return of the Sovereign after visits abroad, and so on. After 1817, the practice of Royal Odes was dropped and gradually the Master's activities faded into inertia (in spite of their £200-a-year stipend) until Sir Edward Elgar (Master for the last ten years of his life) revived them by dedicating his *Nursery Suite* to the young Princesses, Elizabeth and Margaret Rose.

When AB had been knighted in 1950, he had told a friend that his investiture at the Palace had made his feel 'As excited as a small boy on a Prize-Giving Day'[2], such was his respect for royal patronage and ceremonial, so naturally he was delighted to receive this further acknowledgement of his achievements. The appointment of MQM had great prestige, being regarded as the ultimate rung of the official ladder for a British composer, but it would be completely wrong to portray Bliss as a pompous establishment figure. Certainly he was gratified by the honour and certainly his sense of history and awareness of special occasions made him the ideal person to hold the office, but to conclude that it made him swollen-headed would be a great mistake; there was no pretension or self-importance about his character and although he admired tradition he was the opposite of reactionary. He always looked forwards, never backwards.

Bliss lost no time in fulfilling what he considered as one of the duties of his new office. During the early part of the year following her Coronation, the young Queen and her husband

1. Alec Robertson, *Radio Times*, 10.7.53.
2. Edward Liveing, *The Queen*, 10.3.54.

A lesson from Grandfather.

undertook an extended tour of the British Commonwealth and on their return her new Master of Musick was ready with *A Song of Welcome*, scored for two solo singers, mixed chorus and orchestra, which included ceremonial trumpets.[1] The words were specially written by C. Day Lewis and the piece was broadcast on the night of the Queen's return, a prompt and dutiful response by Sir Arthur, totally in character.

Almost exactly a year later Bliss, who had recently become a grandfather for the first time with the arrival of Susan Gatehouse, began the task of fulfilling another commission, that from the Feeney Trust on Behalf of the Birmingham Symphony Orchestra for a major work. He had received a present of a copy of John Blow's *Coronation Anthems* and *Anthems with Strings* in the *Musica Britannica* edition and 'happened to open the volume at the verse anthem "The Lord is my Shepherd"'.[2] Here he found a theme which caught his eye, and ear, providing him with the 'kick start' he needed. He felt that he could use elements of this theme to compose orchestral variations which would illustrate all the verses of Psalm xxiii, and it seemed to him that the title 'Meditations' would give him more freedom than the more formal 'Variations'. This freedom which he sought is exemplified in the music: each 'meditation' contains an element of the main theme but often it is so fleeting, or so camouflaged, as to be unrecognizable at a first hearing; the imagery of each verse in the Psalm, however, is faithfully characterized in the music, so the work should be listened to while following the words even though they are not sung. Bliss had the imaginative idea of keeping John Blow's theme, on which the whole work is loosely based, until the end, instead of stating it at the outset as in most 'theme and variations' compositions. This has the effect of allowing the work to sound like a journey – a sort of 'pilgrim's progress' – with the final destination, 'In the House of the Lord', magnificently portrayed by all the brass playing the theme, with violins accompanying it at a high pitch, ending on a confident chord of attainment. When this *finale* is reached, you feel you have arrived safely in spite of all the dangers encountered on the journey; it is intensely satisfying.

Meditations is one of AB's best orchestral works and should certainly be heard by anyone wishing to appreciate his inventive melodies and brilliant scoring. He very rarely expressed satisfaction with his own compositions but made an exception in this instance: 'If I were to be asked,' he wrote later, 'for a few works that might represent my life's music, this would certainly be one of them.'[3] And this view was echoed by the music critic of *The Times*, writing a few months after the first performance: 'Not since "Enigma" has so fertile an idea for incorporation into variation form been so convincingly worked out.'[4]

1. Craggs, op. cit. p.180.
2. G. Roscow, op. cit. p223.
3. Bliss, op. cit. p195.
4. *The Times*, 'Sir Arthur Bliss – a Modern Romantic' 27.4.56.

The arrival of British musicians in Moscow, 14 April 1956. From left: A Russian hostess, Phyllis Sellick, Leon Goossens, Trudy Bliss, Clarence Raybould, Jennifer Vyvian, AB, Aram Khatchaturyan, two Russian interpreters, Dmitri Kabalevsky (with spectacles).

The same critic, writing in pseudo-Churchillian style, claimed that Bliss was 'In tune with the English tradition', giving as examples *A Colour Symphony* ('... full blooded, attractive music that proclaimed not the doctrinaire but the romantic', *The Olympians* ('... frank opulence of colour'), and *Checkmate*. ('The dramatic side of Bliss's music ... was resoundingly demonstrated in the ballet ...') But, as there was little in these examples to show a distinctively English tradition, the writer compromised by saying that in the last decade Bliss had revealed a 'consolidation of his personal style, which may be roughly described as twentieth century romanticism ...'[1] To be fair, the writer and his newspaper were doing their best to give a boost to contemporary British music and musicians, at a time when Bliss was attempting to do the same thing in Russia.

He had been asked by the British Council to head a party of British musicians on a visit to the USSR, playing concerts in Moscow, Leningrad, Kiev, and Kharkov. The party consisted of Sir Arthur and his wife, Jennifer Vyvian the soprano, Leon Goossens the oboist, the conductor Clarence Raybould, Alfredo Campoli, Cyril Smith and his wife Phyllis Sellick, and the accompanist Gerald Moore – all musicians of renown in Britain but virtually unknown, except for a few recordings, on the other side of the 'iron curtain', as Churchill had described the dividing line between East and West Europe. This was the first cultural visit of its kind behind the 'curtain' since the war and one of its main aims, as AB said, was to 'further the opportunity for others to follow.'[2] It was therefore an important event, from the diplomatic as well as from the musical angle, and the letter of appreciation from the Foreign Office which AB received on their return[3] was

1. *The Times*, ibid.
2. Bliss gives an entertaining account of this tour in *As I Remember* pp196–201, and wrote a factual report for *The Times* published on 1.6.56. pp11–12.
3. Quoted in *As I Remember*, p201.

the formal recognition of its success. But this was not achieved without a tragic slice of human suffering.

Cyril Smith and Phyllis Sellick had formed, before the war, a piano duo of considerable charm and virtuosity, besides continuing their separate careers as soloists, and they gave the first recital of the tour at the large Conservatoire Hall in Moscow. It was very enthusiastically received and seemed to be a good omen for the coming three weeks. Phyllis, however, continued to worry about the tour; for some reason which Cyril could never fathom, she was upset by fear of unexplained danger or disaster.[1] He thought her nervousness was caused by the musical context and apprehension of audience reaction, so when they arrived in Kiev (the third 'leg' of the schedule) he insisted they spent their free time practising on the two pianos at the opera house instead of joining the others who were watching the spectacular May Day celebrations outside. All went well with their concert the following evening: it was a triumphant success like all the others; but the next day they flew on to Kharkov and it was during this journey that Cyril suffered the stroke which was eventually to leave him paralysed in one arm. He was unaware of what had happened at first and on arrival at their hotel asked for a meal of fried chicken and a glass of beer, but it was soon clear that he was a hospital case and the next day that was where the Russian doctor had him taken. Phyllis stayed with him, of course, and after a few days she was joined by Trudy Bliss who detached herself from the rest of the party and remained in Kharkov for two-and-a-half weeks, anxiously hoping for an improvement in Cyril's condition. When this failed to materialize, Trudy flew alone to Moscow and the invalid, with his wife, a nurse and an interpreter, endured an appalling twenty-hour journey by train, being finally greeted by Trudy at Moscow railway-station. The doctor decided that Cyril could fly back to London and while this was being arranged Trudy herself returned home alone. She had a sad story to tell when she arrived but had her own strong sense of duty not induced her to stay with Phyllis and Cyril in Kharkov their plight could have been a good deal more disagreeable.

The story of Cyril Smith's eventual recovery (although only partial) and his brave return to the concert-platform is told in his and his wife's book *Duet for Three Hands*.[2] AB himself later arranged his *Concerto for Two Pianos* for them to play. But if this account of the 1956 tour in Russia seems to have been overshadowed by the illness of Cyril Smith, it should be said that in spite of the natural dismay of Bliss and his party at what had happened, nothing could detract from the warmth of friendship which had been established between them and their Russian counterparts; over three weeks the 'cold war' had experienced a cultural thaw which enabled many exchanges to take place during

1. C. Smith, op. cit. passim.
2. Op. cit.

the next thirty years. AB himself returned to Moscow two years later, at the invitation of Shostakovich, to be a member of the jury of the Tchaikovsky International Competition for Pianists. This visit, on which Trudy accompanied him, was followed by a return one from Shostakovich who was also awarded the Royal Philharmonic Society Gold Medal in 1966; unfortunately he was not well enough to come and receive it from Bliss, who presented it *in absentia*.[1]

Another important aim of this Russian tour had been to arrange a free flow of published music between the two countries, and of course AB was an ideal negotiator, as President of the Performing Right Society, in this objective. He explained the difficulties from the copyright angle to the Minister of Culture but at that time it was very hard to cut across the red tape binding Soviet administration, so in this one respect the mission failed to achieve its purpose fully. As a Russian newspaper reported on the eve of their departure, 'The concerts given by our guest artistes, which were broadcast and televised, were a great success with the Soviet audience, who were glad of the opportunity to meet these gifted musicians from England.'[2]

Bliss was himself entirely convinced of the value of cultural exchanges between countries, of whatever political complexion:

... no musicians could wish for a warmer reception than we got from the concert audiences, consisting mostly of young Russians. Looking from the platform at them was exactly like facing one of our own Promenade Concert audiences.[3]

Now that he was Master of the Queen's Musick, Bliss had many invitations to repeat such visits to other parts of the world but it was not the title or the office which made him such an ideal ambassador for his country, it was his own benign personality and ability to make friends with fellow musicians everywhere, added to his sense of occasion and aptitude for the right words for a speech.

Two years after returning home from the Russian tour, he accepted the honorary post of President of the London Symphony Orchestra and promptly went with them on a short tour of Belgium, including a concert at Ypres, a place which had many memories for him. This visit moved him deeply.[4] After another LSO concert, at the Festival Hall in June 1960, he presented Zoltan Kodaly, the Hungarian composer, with a special tribute from the Orchestra in a speech which clearly gave pleasure equally to both parties. From Harry Dugarde on behalf of the Orchestra, he received a letter thanking him for his '... magnificent contribution to last night's concert. Your speech was more than worthy

1. S. Craggs, op. cit. p40.
2. *News*, A Soviet Review of World Events, 10.5.56. p19.
3. Bliss, op. cit. p199.
4. Bliss, op. cit. p204-5.

Sketch of AB by Joy Finzi, 1955.

of a great occasion and I feel that we are indeed fortunate to have such a fine President!' And from the recipient of the honour, this: 'Dear Sir Arthur, I cannot leave England before sending you a word of thanks, for all you did. Beside and beyond all attractive features of England it is the brother-like behaviour of my colleagues which makes my standing here so agreeable and which I hope to enjoy in future more often than I could the last years. Thanking again with best wishes. Yours very sincerely, Z. Kodaly.'[1]

With all his official engagements and overseas visits, there was less time during the years of the late 1950s for Bliss to devote to composition. However, he fulfilled a commitment to write an Overture for the Edinburgh Festival in 1956 which he based on the city's name, cleverly incorporating its rhythm in his opening chords which recur later in slower tempo; the work is a kaleidoscope of Scottish history, with the middle section devoted to a slow and stately dance in memory of Queen Mary. This is an attractive piece of music, lasting for about ten minutes, which well deserves revival in a concert programme.

The following year saw the production of two very different works, *Discourse for Orchestra* and the score for the British film *Seven Waves Away*. The first was dedicated to the Louisville (Kentucky) Symphony Orchestra, in response to their enterprising commissioning policy, and first performed by them in Louisville.[2] But Bliss completely revised the work (in fact, rewrote it[3]) in 1965 and it was first performed in its new version by AB and the LSO at the Festival Hall in September of that year.[4] On the score, published by Novello, AB wrote quite a comprehensive note explaining the choice of title. He was proud of his ability to participate in a conversation without having to pause and think hard what to say next, so this piece for full orchestra is an illustration of such a 'discourse', in musical terms. At about the time it was originally written, he sometimes shared a joke with his friend Artur Schnabel of indulging in a 'conversation competition' in which each would see for how long he could discourse on a subject without noticeable pause; this harmless pastime *may* have been the origin of *Discourse for Orchestra*.[5] The work was broadcast by the BBC as recently as January 1988, but as far as I know it has never been recorded. The other composition of 1957 – the film score – was not published[6] and appears to have passed into oblivion; the holograph is in the Cambridge University Library.

Early in 1957, Bliss was invited to provide a new work for the University of California, where he had previously taught in

1. Both letters with kind permission of Lady Bliss.
2. S. Craggs, op. cit. p35.
3. Ibid. p94.
4. Bliss, op. cit. p241.
5. I am grateful to Mr George Dannatt for suggesting this possibility.
6. S. Craggs, op. cit. p174.

Guests at the ballet, January 1955: Sir Arthur and Lady Bliss with Dame Ninette de Valois.

the Music Department. The request came from David Boyden who proposed a One-Act ballet score, with which AB agreed.[1] It was left to the composer to choose a scenario for the ballet and this time he decided to develop an idea from his friend Christopher Hassall who suggested 'The Lady of Shalott', the eponymous heroine of Tennyson's poem.[2] The subject attracted AB – he must have felt it would be suitable for the intended event at Berkeley, the ceremonial opening and dedication of some new buildings, but he did tell Boyden that he was taking some 'permissible liberties' with the story while working out the scenario.[3] By mid-summer he was hard at work on the score itself and had completed it by the following February, well within his time-limit. It was first performed by the San Francisco Ballet on 2nd May 1958, but Bliss was not present.

This brief sketch of the birth of a new Bliss work for the stage gives some idea of the brisk and purposeful way he worked; there was still a touch of the old Army Instruction Manual about the approach, perhaps, and a glimpse at the finish of 'that's that, now for the next job', but the core of the assignment – the writing – was accomplished with care and with the greatest attention to the artistic requirements. We can appreciate this creative integrity by

1. Ibid p250.
2. Bliss, op. cit. pp206-7.
3. S. Craggs, op. cit. p251.

watching the video cassette of Bliss and the girls of the New Park School ballet group who were preparing, with the Leicestershire Schools Symphony Orchestra, for a filmed version of the work in 1975. Here was an old man (it was filmed within a very few months of his death) explaining to enthusiastic young amateurs how the music had been conceived and illustrating on the piano – with *panache* – how various phrases should sound, all as if he had been sitting at his own piano eighteen years earlier giving birth to *The Lady of Shalott*. The spellbound reaction of the young people to this remarkable teacher was obvious.

Was this the end for 'The Lady' as AB referred to the work? It was never published, in full score, and neither was the 'Suite' which he arranged from it, but he did send a piano score and scenario of the ballet to Dame Ninette de Valois at the time of composition[1] and it was reported that she was interested in a possible production by the Royal Ballet, if a choreographer could be found to do it justice, but nothing has transpired since.

> For 'ere she reach'd upon the tide
> The first house by the water-side,
> Singing in her song she died,
> The Lady of Shalott.

---

1. S. Craggs, op. cit. p251.

7 Triumphs and Disappointments

> There will be time, there will be time ...
> Time for you and time for me,
> And time for a hundred indecisions,
> And for a hundred visions and revisions ...
>
> *TS Eliot – from 'The Love Song of J Alfred Prufrock'*

In September 1954, Bliss accepted an invitation to become President of the Western Orchestral Society, the body which controlled the Bournemouth Symphony Orchestra. His link with this orchestra had begun many years earlier, in 1922, when Dan Godfrey had asked him to come down to the old Winter Gardens in Bournemouth to conduct his *Rout* and *Two Orchestral Studies*. It was Godfrey's policy to encourage British contemporary composers by performing their music and, if they also conducted – as many did – giving them a chance to present their own works. During the 1922-23 season, for example, thirty-one new British works were given performances in Bournemouth, and thirty-two the following year; there were thirty-one concerts in each season and on ten occasions in each year the composer conducted his own work.[1] These statistics are remarkable evidence of Godfrey's persistence in promoting British contemporary music and the two seasons quoted were not exceptional; there was one winter at the beginning of the century when forty-four new British works were given but then the total number of concerts was sixty.[2]

On this first visit in 1922, Godfrey found AB's music 'problematical but nonetheless interesting'[3] but consoled himself (and possibly the orchestra) with the observation that modern composers were going through '... an experimental period which will adjust itself in due course.'[4] It may be wondered how the audiences in this newly fashionable seaside resort responded to these experiments in modern British music and the answer is probably that they were at least as mystified as the conductor but sufficiently mollified by their loyalty to him and by the inclusion in each programme of several popular favourites to go on supporting these subscription concerts.

In November of the same year, Bliss went to Bournemouth to

1. Stephen Lloyd, *Sir Dan Godfrey, Champion of British Composers*, Thames Publishing, 1995, p224.
2. Ibid.
3. Ibid. p143.
4. Ibid.

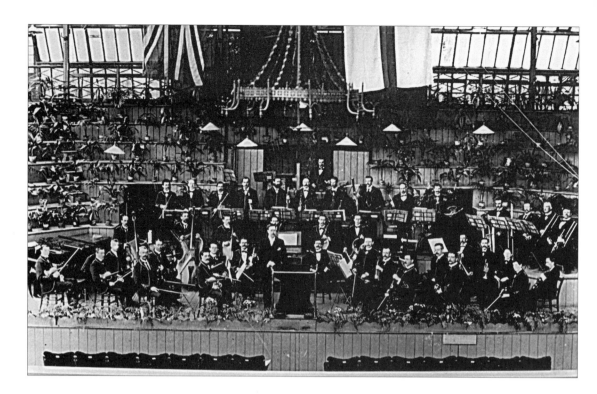

The Bournemouth
Municipal Orchestra in the
'old' Winter Gardens at
Bournemouth; about 1900,
judging by the number of
players and the age of the
conductor, Dan Godfrey.
(Courtesy of 'Bournemouth Orchesras')

conduct his *Colour Symphony* which had had its first – very dis-appointing – performance it may be remembered, in Gloucester Cathedral two months earlier. Godfrey showed his faith in Bliss by promoting this work which had not yet been heard in London, but he and the composer received scant reward from the local press critic who lambasted them both in no uncertain terms. He described it as: '… exceedingly complex, especially in rhythmic details … also a very evident attempt at cleverness, which is a besetting sin of so many young composers … [Bliss is] a poor conductor, and no kind of help could have been gained by the orchestra from such extraordinary "left-handed" cues.'[1]

A Colour Symphony was not heard in Bournemouth again until October 1936,[2] but this did not deter Godfrey from inviting AB's brother, Howard, who had become a music teacher, to be the soloist in Elgar's *Cello Concerto* at a concert in March of the following year, nor AB himself to conduct the first performance of his revised *Concerto for Piano, Tenor Voice and Strings* in the same month.[3] Thereafter, AB's connection with the Bournemouth Orchestra became more tenuous but he did conduct it fairly regu-larly as a Guest Conductor, even after Godfrey's retirement in 1934, and the following notes by a member of the Orchestra during the later years show him to have inspired some affectionate recollections:

1. *Bournemouth Times and Directory* 17.11.22.
2. S. Lloyd, op. cit. p154.
3. S. Lloyd, op. cit. p157.

His dignity, his imperious – but never autocratic – bearing, his breezy
hail-fellow-well-met personality, belong to the Age of Chivalry ... The
Orchestra loves to sit and watch him at work, and to work for him. He
is incredible in his vitality and enthusiasm. It is impossible to believe
that he is past seventy-five. His voice rings out charged with authority
'NO! DON'T *DO* IT!', he roars to some unfortunate player who has
anticipated an entry, 'WAIT for the beginning of the six-eight bar!'

Or sensing a little slackness towards the back desks of one of the string
sections: 'Now then – pull your socks up there – we must all be very
neat at this point you know!'

His bright eyes twinkle as he surveys his troops. He settles well back
on his rehearsal seat, both arms raised and stretched forward, baton at
an angle. 'Now we'll take the slow movement. Relax a bit I don't want
you to strain after the effect as long as you keep the rhythm nicely defined
and neat. Mind that quaver rest on the third beat it must be felt quite
clearly I don't want any loose ends tagging over. Right – are we ready?
And take it easy. Three-four ...' And we are off ...

One of my colleagues in the wind section recently, playing yet another
performance of 'A Colour Symphony' with Sir Arthur at rehearsal,
entirely missed his entry for a rather important solo passage. 'Now, now
– come along', gently remonstrated the conductor 'take it again from
four bars after letter K'. My friend 'took it again' but told me afterwards
that he was so spell-bound in watching the way Sir Arthur was working,
admiring his freshness, energy and vitality, that he completely forgot
again to 'come in'. It was not surprising.

At one of our away-dates, I came upon Sir Arthur sitting quietly
behind the scenes about half an hour before the concert was due to start,
soft hat well tilted back upon his head, silk scarf around his neck, a

glowing cigarette held nonchalantly between his fingers. He looked at peace with all the world, a spark of anticipatory pleasure glinting in his eyes.

'I wonder what you would say,' I said to him, 'if I were to ask you how you manage to look so lively, so fit, always. To what do you attribute it?'

'Ha!' he replied, 'do I then? Well, you know I've always worked hard – I like work. I think it does you good. I'm always working. And then, of course, I've got five grandchildren – and I think they keep me young.'[1]

One rather surprising fact about Bliss's Bournemouth connection, in view of its help to him at the start of his career, is that he did not mention it in *As I Remember*, although he was generous in his gratitude to Henry Wood for the encouragement he received from him as a young man. Perhaps he forgot that Godfrey's support for British music of the twentieth century was at least as comprehensive as Wood's and given over a longer period. But there is no doubt about AB's repayment of the debt he owed to Godfrey. He described the 'new' Orchestra which emerged from the founding of the Western Orchestral Society as 'the bright phoenix-bird' and gave it all the help he could; in 1959, for example, he conducted it in a concert at the restored Portsmouth Guildhall.

It is interesting to have a glimpse of how orchestral players see a conductor at work, especially one so extrovert as Arthur Bliss. Some famous conductors of the past have been so self-conscious that their gestures and facial expressions were more suited to a mime-show than a concert-hall and their bizarre contortions can have had little or no effect on how their orchestras played the music in front of them. Bliss was not one of these, nor did he want to be:

Three Sellick grandchildren (and AB) in Trafalgar Square.

Some conductors ... have a third eye somewhere in the back of their heads, which keeps an unwinking gaze on the audience's attention and reactions. I just hope I am not one of them.[2]

AB's reference to 'five grandchildren' was rather parsimonious; he did, in fact, have six – probably the youngest, Laura, was born after this conversation took place. His younger daughter, Karen, had married Christopher Sellick in 1956 and, like his elder daughter Barbara, she had three children, all girls. In 1963 the Sellick family emigrated to Perth, Australia, and the following year AB and Trudy flew out there to stay near them for two months. During that time, AB flew to Sydney to take part in the first of four concerts arranged by The British Council. In the programme, he included his own *Music for Strings* together with other chamber works by Purcell, Vaughan Williams and Britten, played by the Sydney Little Symphony Orchestra. From Sydney he flew to Brisbane for two concerts, which included his *Colour Symphony*

1. Miss D. Maxwell, with kind permission.
2. Bliss, op. cit. p235.

Two of the Gatehouse grandchildren with their grandparents.

and *The Beatitudes* (see p102), then back to Perth for one more concert before he and Trudy left Australia – and their family – to visit Japan. There were pre-arranged concerts in Tokyo, Kyoto and Osaka given by the LSO, conducted by Istvan Kertesz and Colin Davis, their President conducting his own *Colour Symphony* and dances from *Checkmate*. But when these engagements were successfully concluded, AB and Trudy could at last relax and enjoy the rest of their 'holiday'. Before returning home, they spent a few restful weeks in Hong Kong and Ceylon (Sri Lanka), enjoying all the sights, especially of Kandy and Nuwara Eliya. Both were keen plant and bird lovers and they enjoyed the exotic but peaceful nature reserves of the Far East as much as they appreciated oriental peoples and cultures. There is a full and entertaining description of this three-month tour in *As I Remember*[1] but we must now turn back to 1960 and to Bliss's compositions as he approached his seventieth birthday.

Television as a medium for drama and music inevitably attracted Bliss; its direct transmission to people's homes has an immediacy which appealed to his character and his experience with writing film-music prompted ideas for the small screen. His first commission was for some short excerpts to accompany a BBC series of Shakespeare's historical plays (from Richard II to Richard III) called *An Age of Kings*. The music, consisting of a Prelude, Chorale and Postlude, lasted in total for less than seven minutes but it was played by the Royal Philharmonic Orchestra and conducted by Lionel Salter.[2] He and AB had first met during

1. Chapter XXIV.   2. Foreman, 'Catalogue', p75.

Sir Arthur Bliss accepting a
gold medal from the Deputy
Governor of Tokyo on behalf
of the LSO. With him are
Colin Davis and Ernest
Fleischmann. November
1964.

the making of the film *Things to Come*, and they had formed a
healthy admiration for each other. Salter was now Head of Music
for BBC Television and was thus in a position to commission
another TV work from Bliss: *Tobias and the Angel*.

For this two-act opera, AB again co-opted Christopher Hassall
for the script and they chose, from the apocryphal 'Book of Tobit',
a dramatic story with strong moral and supernatural undertones.
Rudolph Cartier was the producer and Norman del Mar the
conductor, with the LSO and a strong cast of singers.[1] The opera
was broadcast on 19 May 1960, and Mr Salter tells me that some
of the special effects were later used in the long-running BBC
drama, *Doctor Who*. He adds that his admiration of AB's character
was further increased when, during production, he had to tell him
that all the short passages the composer had written linking one
scene with another would have to be scrapped as they were
unnecessary: 'Never mind,' AB replied, 'just do it.'[2]

The music does, in fact, join the short scenes together smoothly
and, as in *The Olympians*, it represents the changing moods of the
drama very effectively. Again, the composer employs a full
orchestra and uses all its tone-colours productively; the harp is
conspicuous in some of the love-music. But in contrast to *The*

1. Foreman, op cit. p74.
2. Mr L. Salter, with kind permission.

The garden scene from the television opera *Tobias and the Angel*, May 1960.
(Photo, the BBC)

Olympians, the music for this shorter opera is less obtrusively operatic: in short, simpler in style. Ironically, Bliss was criticized, after the first performance was screened, for writing some completely banal music to accompany a song which the character Azarias (in fact, the Archangel Raphael) is singing while gutting a fish; it occurs twice more, always at moments when the true identity of Azarias is crucial to the drama. Bliss defended the use of this simple tune on the grounds that a 'quiet chorale-like melody' was entirely appropriate for the character of an Archangel and that 'It came like a flash into my mind when I first read the words.'[1] One feels that he was totally justified: the music *is* appropriate, and simplicity (of high quality) has never let an operatic composer down yet.

The work was dedicated to Trudy Bliss and won an award of Merit when it was later repeated at a Festival in Salzburg[2] but unfortunately it has not been seen again on British television; nor has the stage version – which Bliss arranged and Novello published – been produced by 'some enterprising opera company', as Bliss hoped it would be.[3]

1. Roscow, op. cit. p368.
2. Bliss, op. cit. p208.
3. Bliss, op cit. p208.

Lionel Salter recording the music for *An Age of Kings*, with AB and the Producer, March 1960. (Photo, the BBC)

During the production of these two works, *An Age of Kings* and *Tobias*, Salter and Bliss spent a good deal of time together, driving to and from the studios at Denham or BBC recording sessions. On one evening, with Trudy sitting in the back of the car and AB driving, they came through a town when the cinemas were closing and people who had just come out were thronging the road. Salter thought AB was driving dangerously close to them and uttered a caution but a rather tired voice from the back said, 'Oh, don't worry him, Lionel, Arthur's always so gregarious.' Another time, AB and Salter were alone together in the car – again in the evening – when they passed two youths fighting on the pavement; one had an iron bar and was starting to lay into the other with it. AB immediately stopped the car, walked over to them and calmly disarmed the youth before returning to the car in the same leisurely fashion. But where music was concerned, Salter insists, AB was 'the ultimate professional, never at a loss for words of advice when asked.' As a conductor, he recalls, AB was obviously not a 'Maestro', in any sense but 'the players respected him, enjoyed his jokes and never played tricks with him as they occasionally did with some other conductors.'[1]

When AB celebrated his seventieth birthday on 2 August 1961, he was naturally asked by many journalists, as the premier figure in British music, for 'words of advice' which were widely reported in the press. Some of these reports make interesting reading thirty-five years later because they include, typically, comments which were almost prophetic in their time and pose questions which are as apt today as they were then. Here are a few short extracts:

1. Mr L. Salter, with kind permission.

I emphasize the *ear* [talking of Webern's *Five Movements for String Quartet*] because that is my only criterion for judging music and I doubt whether the ear of today is yet rightly equipped for assess-ing a great deal of the music now written. The 'still small voice' of Webern is a wonderful corrective to unformed noise, but how can the ear function both as an excluder and as a concentrator? ... Once a work is really heard, so that it remains in the mind and on the fingers, analysis can add to the pleasure. Analysing without the ability really to hear is just using music as a crossword exercise.[1]

His music is never heard today. [talking of Bernard van Dieren] Why? Are we in music bound to the wheel of fashion as firmly as dress designers?[2]

Other writers preferred to use the occasion of Bliss's seventieth birthday to present their own opinions about his music in relation to contemporary trends:

His work is not mentioned in a book published only four years ago dealing with music in the present century. Young men, pale with atonalism, look down on him because he is Master of the Queen's Music, and likes to spell 'music' with a k. Yet this same Arthur Bliss was rather regarded as a rebel 40 years ago, and remains forward-looking as a man and as artist. He has composed one of the first television operas; his film music stands with the best in point of vivid atmospheric, picturesque, and dramatic aptness. He is in harness yet, composing music which, whether his critics may approve of it or not, is certain to be signed by his own eclectic manner and individuality ... His music is always virile, masculine, and the main factor in his individual style is a definite objective way of expressing his emotional, thinking, and seeing processes. He has done much to 'slim' English music, and to free instru-mental character and timbre from the thick texture prevalent during his heyday. At the present time his music sounds confident, even breezy. Consequently it is for the time being not accepted in the new Estab-lishment ... None the less, only a narrow and partisan culture, such as ours at the moment, could consistently neglect works as individually conceived and as expertly composed as the Oboe Quintet, the engaging and versatile 'Pastoral', the eloquent, deeply-felt 'Morning Heroes', and 'Music for Strings'.[3]

Another well known music critic dwelt on Sir Arthur's per-sonality in relation to his post as MQM:

No one knows exactly what is expected from a Master of the Queen's Music, but at moments of national focus we turn to him expectantly all the same. In Sir Arthur Bliss, who is 70 this week, we encounter just the paradoxical figure necessary to make the post of anything more than figurehead value. A Rugbeian ex-Grenadier, he cuts a figure reassuring in St James's but is keenly interested in the latest composing affairs.

1. Quoted by Henry Raynor, 'Recollections for a Birthday', *Daily Telegraph*, 29.7.61.
2. Ibid.
3. Neville Cardus, 'The Venerable Square', *The Guardian*, 2.8.61.

101

His carefully written speeches, uttered in that rather high, military voice, are 'suitable' but full of thought: he will use official occasions calling for compliments to make serious pleas on music's behalf, and be prepared to leave significant gaps in the compliments. He is the spokesman who can quietly put a spoke in the wheel, and he has never lost his curiosity.

Those who were responsible for choosing Bliss as Master presumably ignored this last quality. Curiosity is not a virtue highly regarded by British officialdom. But it has actually proved more useful to him in his various official duties than as a composer, where it seems partly to have been the expression of more uncertainty than the confident surface of his music suggests.[1]

At the time these tributes were written, Bliss was hard at work on his latest important commission, a large choral and orchestral work. He wrote later:

As soon as I had received the invitation to contribute a work for the opening of the new Cathedral at Coventry – to be celebrated in May 1962 – I asked Christopher Hassall to come to London ... and talk over possible subjects that would suit the occasion. It was *his* suggestion that the Nine Beatitudes should be the theme.[2]

As he studied the implications of this idea Bliss felt that he would need to introduce interludes which provided complete contrasts to the theme of Blessing which inspires the words of Jesus in St Matthew's Gospel. The composition would thus involve several outbursts of violence – 'force opposing the beatific vision'[3] – to relieve monotony. In this scheme for the work, there is a clear implication that Bliss had in mind the resounding acoustic properties of a large church, or cathedral, for its performance. How else would these startling contrasts be achieved?

I had been led to believe that the performance was to take place in the majestic surroundings of the new Cathedral, but alas! the Cathedral was needed for services and the concert was relegated to the Coventry (Belgrade) Theatre, a maladjustment most unfortunate to me.[4]

The euphemism of this last phrase, so typical of AB's modesty, conceals a colossal affront by the Coventry Cathedral Festival Committee. The composer, a deeply sensitive man beneath his bluff exterior, was not just being denied the prestige of having his Cantata performed in the great new building, recently consecrated – a rejection he would have borne with dignity – but he was forced to conduct it in conditions which ensured its failure at this first performance. The stage of the theatre was too small to accommodate the large orchestra and chorus; the small portable electric organ was hopelessly inadequate for the part it had

1. John Warrack, 'Mastering the Queen's Music', *Sunday Telegraph*, 30.7.61.
2. Bliss, op. cit. p209.
3. Ibid.
4. Bliss, op. cit. p.212.

to play; above all, the soft acoustic of the upholstered theatre deadened the musical and dramatic effects which were intrinsic to the work and which the composer had taken great trouble to invent.

'Sacred music but in a secular atmosphere'[1] was *The Times* head-line the next day after the performance and the criticism which followed was inevitably adverse: the work lacked

... the spaciousness and the mystery of atmosphere that a church will give ... the slender coherence of the whole cantata is also, one suspects, caused by a preponderance of musical invention that is merely suitable and not spiritually inevitable ...

It is possible, even likely, that an inspired performance, with superb choral singing, will raise these apparently weaker sections to the level of the finer ones. Such a performance might even remove the niggling fear that Bliss had intended a challenging call to a Christian and chari-table way of life but lacked the courage to sound the clarion as fervently and uncompromisingly as the message demands.[2]

In the previous day's *Times* there was a long preview of Britten's specially composed *War Requiem* which ended: 'There is no doubt at all, even before next Wednesday's performance, that it is Britten's masterpiece.'[3]

Bliss would never have claimed as much for *The Beatitudes* and would have heartily agreed with the verdict on Britten's great work (however premature he might have thought it) but there is no doubt about his profound disappointment with the fate of his own cantata:

The reviews on the work hoped that a performance would be given in the Cathedral, its rightful place, on 'The earliest possible occasion after the Festival'. As I write six years later, this expectancy remains unful-filled.[4]

(There was, however, a second performance at Gloucester Cathedral the following September and it was performed in London six months later.)

Bliss was delighted to receive, early the following year, the Gold Medal of the Royal Philharmonic Society. Having previously presented it to four other recipients, 'To receive it now myself ... gave me great delight.'[5] In his speech of thanks, he included this touching remark:

I don't claim to have done more than light a small taper at the shrine of music. I do not upbraid Fate for not having given me greater gifts. In the endeavour has been the joy.[6]

1. *The Times*, 26.5.62.
2. Ibid.
3. *The Times*, 24.5.62.
4. Bliss, op. cit. p212.
5. Ibid.
6. Quoted by J.B. in 'Bon Papa – an interview with Sir Arthur Bliss', *Youth and Music News*, July 1963.

The Cheltenham International Festival of Music: a formal part of the Festival in July, 1971. From left: AB, the Mayoress of Cheltenham, A. Crabtree (Festival Secretary), the Mayor, Lady Bliss, F. Howes (Music critic of *The Times*).
(Photo by John Cheesman, Cheltenham)

As so often before, Bliss followed a large-scale composition (*The Beatitudes*) with a chamber work *A Knot of Riddles*, commissioned by the BBC for the 1963 Cheltenham Festival. The motivation this time came from some translations of the medieval Exeter Book (by K. Crossley-Holland) which AB had read in *The Listener*. He chose seven conundrums and set them for solo baritone and ten instruments, the answer to each one being partly guessable by the realism of the music but, as one writer has observed, '... the answers are given by the same soloist, generally followed by a pertinent orchestral comment or, in two cases, by silence almost more telling and more laughter producing.'[1] In short, this was a light-hearted frolic for a Festival which was also close to AB's heart and he must have enjoyed writing it. Two years later, he was elected President of the Cheltenham International Festival of Music, which he had attended since its inauguration in 1945 (as a Festival of British Contemporary Music). He and Trudy greatly enjoyed the informal – but well informed – atmosphere of this annual event which now attracts literature, art and music-lovers from many parts of the world. His long and faithful association with it was recognized in the season after his death when fifteen of his works were performed (together with all fifteen of Shostakovitch's string quartets).

1. George Dannatt, op. cit. p23.

In April 1963, Bliss was greatly saddened by the death of his friend and collaborator Christopher Hassall. Their last work together had just been completed and Bliss dedicated it to his memory. *Mary of Magdala* is another sacred cantata (like *The Beatitudes* but shorter) based on the Gospel story of Mary Magdalene going to the sepulchre three days after Christ's burial, meeting the risen Lord and mistaking him for the gardener. Set for solo contralto (Mary) and bass (Christus), chorus and small orchestra, this gentle and intensely human story brought out some of the best in Bliss's store of melodious and peaceful music. There are no violent interruptions to the narrative but the drama, when Mary finds the tomb empty, is achieved by three bars of vintage Bliss *fortissimo*, ending on a held chord of searing dissonance and followed by some spine-chilling soft and slow music as Mary sees the two angels who have been guarding the tomb and, mistaking them for 'terrible spirits of the dead', thinks she is in a haunted garden. As they reveal themselves and tell her not to weep, the angels (sung by boys' voices) are accompanied by one of Bliss's favourite rhythmic devices, a duplet (two notes in this case syncopated) and a third tied to a triplet (three notes occupying one beat), which might be recognizable thus: da' *aah* da a'a'a'. The effect, under a calm melody in the treble, is one of reassuring expectancy – exactly what the situation in the narrative requires.

The Cantata was first performed at Worcester Cathedral, as part of the Three Choirs Festival, in September 1963, and later in Hull, but it does not appear to have been recorded. It was published in that year by Novello and reprinted in 1969.[1] It is hard to understand why this work has been neglected for so long because it has many virtues: aptness to its context, ease of listening, moderate resources, and, in addition, its length (just under half an hour) which would make it a very good pendant to another Easter-tide work.

To complete a trio of cantatas composed at about this time, Bliss responded to a request from his old University at Cambridge for a work to celebrate the quincentenary of the award of Degrees in Music, Cambridge being the first University to have done so, in 1464. The work he wrote was *The Golden Cantata*; its sub-title 'Music in the Golden Form' – gives a better clue to the composer's intentions but whether it also encompassed the aims of the poet, Kathleen Raine, is open to question. In her letters, which Bliss received her permission to publish,[2] she was unspecific about a direct relationship between her poems and the concept of music as a 'golden form' (or, '*the* golden form' which are the words she herself wrote in the last poem of the set, an ode to music). However, when, after a problem in finding a suitable title, AB suggested the name *Golden Cantata*, she agreed by saying it was 'perfect'[3] The term had been used before in a musical connotation: 'Golden

1. Foreman, 'Catalogue' op. cit. p49.
2. Bliss, op. cit. pp220–224.
3. Bliss, op. cit. p222.

Sonata' was applied to one of Purcell's 'Sonatas in Four Parts' – a particularly beautiful one; one 'Golden Sequence' was a description of a part of the Roman Catholic liturgy sung at Whitsuntide to a particularly beautiful plainsong; 'The Golden Legend', a poem by Longfellow, was the basis of the libretto used by Sullivan in his secular Oratorio of that name, which he thought was his best work.[1] Bliss undoubtedly admired Raine's poetry for its delicacy and sensitivity, although he admitted she was 'not an easy poet to comprehend',[2] so he made a précis of these 'golden' poems in his own words which he thought would help singers in a chorus '... to a comprehension of her theme.'[3] This interpretation does help in a general understanding of the libretto but, as Bliss agreed, the poet's frequent changes of direction in the reasoning between each poem do not make the work easy to follow.

However, his fascination with Kathleen Raine's poetry persisted and four years after *The Golden Cantata* he set another seven poems from her collection in a song-cycle for soprano voice and piano which he called *Angels of the Mind*. In his programme note, he explained that the title is a reference to 'angels both terrible and comforting'[4] which appear in Raine's verses as they did in the poetry of Rilke. Miss Raine's angels seem to have been less dispiriting than Rilke's because she welcomes them in her own experience of life – solitary as that had often been. There was an element of mysticism in the Cycle which must have appealed to Bliss. It is remarkable that a personality so evidently direct and categorical could absorb thoughts so opposite in character as Miss Raine's – not just absorb them but reproduce them in musical dress. One theory is that his personality grew more 'tranquilly urbane' with age and 'discovered the secret of canalizing the excitement of deep emotion into art.'[5] If that is correct, his collaboration with Kathleen Raine must have played a part in the process.

Bliss considered that his personality had changed little over the years and that, having discovered at school how to conceal his true feelings behind a mask of indifference, he used it – the mask – during the next years of his life when he was in the army: '... it enabled me, when I had endured these, to shake off the experiences that might have greatly affected me, and emerge again for my destined life in music as I really was.'[6]

He confesses to feeling occasional moods of dejection in his art, varied with contrary moods of elation, just as any other creative artist might feel, but there the introspection ends. When he asks the question, how can he judge what he is and what he has done, he retreats behind the mask and claims, rightly, that his auto-

---

1. When Sullivan gave a copy of the score to Ethel Smyth and asked her if she agreed, she had the temerity to say she thought *The Mikado* was his masterpiece; he laughed and called her a wretch.
2. Bliss ibid. p219.
3. Ibid.
4. Bliss, op. cit. p290.
5. Henry Raynor, op. cit. 29.7.61.
6. Bliss, op. cit. p239.

'I only feel myself in action ...' – AB with Muir Mathieson, about 1965.

biography '... aims at being mainly factual, showing the kind of life I have led from year to year, and offering a good many letters ...'[1]

Perhaps, if we put together the 'theory' of Henry Raynor and the 'mask confession' of AB, we can begin to draw a sketch of this intriguing personality: a deeply emotional young man who had the mature sense to conceal his emotions when circumstances made it prudent to do so; a confident man in middle age, after his marriage, who knew exactly what his ambition was in life; a sophisticated man in old age who could afford to remove his 'mask' occasionally when emotions could be channelled into the stream of his art. A sketch is only a sketch and no doubt others could add revealing touches to complete the picture.

But it is more than likely that AB himself would have declined to make such additions, had he been asked. He was too reserved about his own personality to want to expose it further than he did in his autobiography: 'My temperament demands activity, not a passive role: I only feel myself in action.'[2]

And he seldom wanted to talk much about his own music, even to close friends: 'For a creative artist there is an unanswered question because there is always an alternative way of doing things.'[3]

'In action ... Doing things ...' those terms certainly emphasised two highlights of AB's personality, and another meaningful term was 'life-enhancing' (a favourite expression of his[4]) meaning that every major act should aim to improve the quality of life, not always for oneself, sometimes for many others. This Platonic ideal was probably culled from many sources but that it had crystallized

1. Bliss, op. cit. p240.
2. Bliss, op. cit. p239.
3. George Dannatt, with kind permission.
4. Karen Sellick, with kind permission.

into one of his aims seems to be borne out by his frequent use of the term. How did he put it into practice? One example was his willingness to take part in a non-profit housing association scheme to provide homes for elderly people at rents they could afford, the Samaritan Housing Association. The first house to be built was at Lindfield, Sussex, and was named 'Arthur Bliss House', in appreciation of his services at a concert in London in aid of the Fund and of his 'general contribution to the world of music'. This gave him great pleasure and, typically, he and Trudy went down to Lindfield when the house was built to meet the occupants (it contained a number of independent flats) and thank them for the compliment paid them.

Many other overt examples of Bliss practising his principle of 'enhancing life' for others are apparent in *As I Remember*: his tireless work for all the organizations of which he was Honorary President or Chairman; his constant interest in young musicians and the practical encouragement he gave them by conducting or attending their concerts – for example, the Orpington Junior Singers, of which he was President. He wrote several songs for this Choir and its conductor, Sheila Mossman, and when she died he composed the very beautiful setting of the 'Prayer of St Francis of Assisi' in her memory. Nor did he forget, in his encouragement of youth, former connections in America: early in 1968 he was asked – and agreed – to compose a 'Fanfare' for the Band of Lehigh University, Pennsylvania, which they could play at a football game against their main rivals, Lafayette College. His friend, Jonathan Elkus, was Professor of Music at the University, so AB wrote the fanfare in short score and sent it with this message: 'If, when you receive it, you feel it may lose you in the game, you must on no account play it.'[1] Elkus scored it for full military band and it didn't lose them the game; AB and Trudy were present on this occasion (they were visiting the State in November that year) and she clearly recalls the mood of rejoicing when they travelled back with the team after the match, being regaled with songs of triumph (in modified versions one hopes).[2]

One last example of the 'life enhancing' theme: when Bliss was asked to contribute a hymn for *The Cambridge Hymnal* of 1967, he chose to set a poem by George Herbert – 'Sweet day, so cool, so calm, so bright' – and named the Tune 'Penselwood' in honour of the place which had lent such enhancement to his own and his family's lives.

The encouragement which AB gave to young musicians was emphasized by Benjamin Britten in a wonderfully warm letter of congratulation on his seventy-fifth birthday – 'Few of our juniors have not been helped directly or indirectly by your practical benevolence.'[3] The letter ends '... since you are the youngest 75 imaginable, (we) look forward confidently to many more years

1. S. Craggs, op. cit. p289.
2. Lady Bliss, with kind permission.
3. Letter to Bliss from B. Britten, dated 4.8.66, by kind permission of Lady Bliss.

of tireless energy and sane guidance.'[1]

Did Bliss himself feel 'the youngest 75 imaginable'? At the end of *As I Remember*, which he began writing earlier in his seventy-fifth year, he wrote:

Do I feel my full weight of years? I cannot say that I do ... It is true that I find my ability to concentrate is now less, and my joy in writing music on the wane ... but I certainly do not feel old age dragging at my heels. I felt indeed positively youthful on August 2nd 1966, when I celebrated my seventy-fifth birthday ...[2]

That birthday was celebrated by a special concert in his honour at the Albert Hall, at which he conducted, and by messages of congratulation from friends and admirers in many parts of the world, including a telegram from the Queen and another, in Russian, from Dmitri Shostakovich. As the following chapter will show, he certainly *cannot* have felt 'old age dragging at his heels'.

1. Ibid.
2. Bliss, op. cit. p246.

8 Olympus Surmounted

> I love all beauteous things;
> I seek and adore them;
> God hath no better praise,
> And man in his hasty days
> Is honoured for them.
>
> *Robert Bridges, from an untitled poem.*

The autobiography *As I Remember* took the story of Arthur Bliss's life up to 1966, when he was seventy-five. It was published (by Faber and Faber) in 1970 and very well received by the reviewers. To give one example:

This is, in short, a memorable book, rich in insight and artistic values. It should become a classic of British musical biography.[1]

Above all, it is an enjoyable book, easy to read and without any trace of self-justification; it is an honest and unadorned account of his interesting life and work. However, the question it leaves specifically unanswered is, what was the true nature of the man behind the public personality?

In April 1974, the last year of his life, Granada Television recorded archival material of AB introducing his *Meditations on a Theme of John Blow* at the piano, an extract of which was published posthumously. It was re-printed in *Bliss on Music* under the title of 'A Testament'; here are some extracts:

I think most people like to feel that they leave behind them a remembrance of a definite personality – hence the photos, portraits, biographies, autobiographies; but in the case of an artist it's a little different, because what he wants to leave behind is his work – the poet his verses, the sculptor his works of art, the painter his canvases, the musician his scores; and of course, there is a reason for this, because with an artist, very often the outer persona that he shows to the world is very different from the inward man at work on his art ... in many cases the composer is a man of two beings – one which perhaps, for self-preservation, he shows the world, the other he keeps hidden and it is only behind the closed door of his workroom that he is really himself, and possibly only his nearest and dearest, in this case my wife, for instance, can blend the two. I have indeed written an autobiography detailing my life to the age of 75, but whoever wants to know the *real* me must listen to my music ...[1]

1. *Musical Times*.
2. G. Roscow, op. cit. pp281-2.

These extracts show very clearly that he was well aware, near the end of his life, that he had *not* revealed the 'inward man' in his autobiography, that he had concealed it intentionally, and that he wished it to be revealed only in his music. A biographer might therefore be tempted to leave it at that. But would it be enough for a book about a musician's life and times, to leave the subject's 'inward man' concealed in his art?

It may be that at least part of the answer has already been given. Perhaps you may feel that enough of the 'inward man' has emerged implicitly in the previous chapters and illustrations to satisfy curiosity about Arthur Bliss's inner persona and that any further attempt to define it would be mere speculation. If so, this writer would be content.

One important area of British music during the last decade of Bliss's life has not yet been discussed – 'pop' music. In June 1971, Bliss made a speech at a dinner held by the Royal Academy of Music Club of which he was an honorary Fellow of the RAM:

I think I am pretty safe in suggesting that at no time in the history of our civilization has music played so prominent a part in our daily life as it does today. In my own field of composition, for instance, it may astonish you to learn that nearly 5000 composers are now elected members of the Performing Right Society ... This tremendous activity is to be commended if it enables the young to construct rather than to destroy, to learn how to express themselves rather than to live in a nagging frustration.

... I believe two dominating and certainly new incentives have contributed to this increasing wish to enter the musical profession. I am not saying that they are the most altruistic ones, only that they have injected a new element into the musical scene. One is money, and the other is glamour ... I remember so well Elgar telling me rather bitterly of his struggles in his early years due to lack of means, and indeed, at the start of this century any young man or young woman who aspired to be a composer without a private income was regarded either as mad or suicidal ... Today, owing to performing fees, commissions, prizes, films, etc. and the relative ease in getting his music heard, a gifted young composer with a modicum of luck can make a living by his own talents, often a very considerable one. This feeling of relief has been a blessing to many composers today.

Referring once more to the 5,000 listed British composers, Bliss continued:

Of course only a small minority of these can be called serious composers. Most of them write pop music (often in groups) or mood music to be heard as a soothing background in airports, factories, bedrooms, etc., or jingles in advertisements ... I am reluctant to use the word 'serious' music, and it is regrettble that for convenience sake we now divide creative achievement into the three categories of serious, light, and pop – because, in reality, all worthwhile music is the result of hard concentrated work and the desire for as perfect a result as possible.

... Composition today is in a strange state ... Side by side with masterworks written since the last war are pieces of extreme silliness, often insulting to an adult audience, and certainly an outrage to musical instruments.

111

It *is* necessary for every new generation to protest and rebel – we have in our time all done it – but it is no use protesting and rebelling when *everything is permitted*. You cannot rebel, with satisfaction, against anarchy, only against some kind of order which you dislike. Now some definition of order is at the very basis of composition ... It must be difficult to teach composition today when the student finds himself unwilling, or indeed unable, to subject himself to disciplined routine. He won't understand that the disciplined routine will give him all the necessary technique and facility, and also give him just the irritant against which he can then rebel.

Finally, Bliss identified:

... the strongest reason why the young want to be musicians, and that, of course, is for the sheer love of it. To an outsider on some other planet it might appear extraordinary that a man or woman could devote their whole lives just to musical sound, but so compulsive is the pull, on this earth, that here we are – all doing it.[1]

The whole text of the speech is well worth reading but perhaps these extracts are sufficient to convey at least two aspects of AB's nature, his understanding of young 'pop' musicians on the one hand and on the other, his certainty that their branch of the art needed self-discipline. He did appreciate the motives of young musicians but he also knew that without self-imposed discipline they couldn't succeed and he was not afraid to say so. The 'swinging sixties' he could sympathize with, the 'permissive society' he could not. Such views were commonly held by many of the older generation at the time but to hear the Master of the Queen's Musick expressing sympathy with the protest and rebellion of youth must have been surprising to any who had never heard of *Rout, Conversations,* or *Madam Noy.* This is what makes AB such an unusual character; he may appear to be a blimp but he turns out, after some examination, to be a youthful dynamo. Invested as a Knight Commander of the Victorian Order in the New Year Honours List of 1967, he flew off to the USA four months later to be elected an honorary member of the American Bible Society. Such diverse characteristics in one individual as these honours imply reveals, at the age of seventy-eight, someone of quite remarkable richness – not a type but a mixture, '... a very human, complex, sensitive and resilient spirit.'[2]

In June 1969, the first performance took place at Blythburgh Parish Church, as part of the Aldeburgh Festival, of Bliss's Cantata *The World is Charged with the Grandeur of God.* He had always wanted to compose a work for this Festival and was glad to be asked by Peter Pears to set three poems by Gerard Manley Hopkins, friend of Robert Bridges who was his literary executor. It was a slightly strange commission in that Bliss's work was to be performed in a concert of music written by 'The Over Seventies' (including Haydn and Verdi!) and he was restricted in its orchestration to the instruments available, which did not include

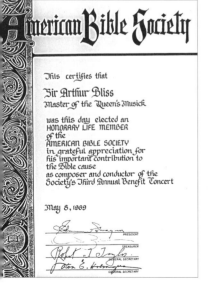

AB's Certificate of Hon. Life Membership of the American Bible Society.

1. Roscow, op. cit. pp275-77.
2. G. Easterbrook, Foreword to S. Craggs, op. cit. pxiv.

112

strings. He therefore scored the first and last poems for mixed chorus and brass, and the middle one for women's voices and two flutes. Another catastrophe dogged the first performance: the Maltings, the concert hall at Snape where most of the Festival's large events were held, was destroyed by fire a few days beforehand. This time, however, the alternative venue of the church may have been rather more suited to Bliss's work than the original one.

The cantata was well received and it was not long before a second Bliss work was heard for the first time at Aldeburgh. This was his *Concerto for Cello and Orchestra*, originally planned back in 1968 as a 'Concertino' (small concerto). Bliss then received a letter from Benjamin Britten saying that Rostropovich had told him in America that he would like to play the work at Aldeburgh in June 1970, a proposal which was eagerly accepted by the composer.[1] He called this a '... light-hearted work, at any rate in the first and third movements ...'[2] but one wonders if perhaps that was the original conception and whether it became a larger – and slightly heavier – work as Bliss converted the piano score into full score. That is only conjecture, but it is certain that Rostropovich was determined to edit the solo part before the full scoring was completed and that must have had its effect, in the same way that Tertis influenced the *Sonata for Viola and Piano*. Even so, the scoring was for quite a small orchestra (Bliss called it 'Mozartian') with the addition of harp and celesta. Britten, who conducted the first performance, called it 'a major work' and persuaded Bliss to designate it a 'Concerto'. More importantly, it is a remarkably virile piece of music, one which is stamped with the Bliss

1. S. Craggs, op. cit. p236.   2. G. Roscow, op. cit. p272.

113

The Investiture of the Prince
of Wales at Caernarfon
Castle, 1969.

'signature' – to anyone who knows it – but which might have
been written by a young man, to anyone who knew nothing to
the contrary. The last movement, especially, is very sparkling and
dynamic, demanding extreme agility from the soloist and players;
in fact, Bliss himself summed up the whole work when he said in
his programme-note for the première: 'There are no problems for
the listener – only for the soloist!'[1]

Virtuosity was certainly an aspect of music which Bliss greatly
admired, from the time he first heard a great American orchestra
demonstrating this quality in the 1920s and throughout his
life. Consequently, he never spared performers of his own music
whether they were singers or instrumentalists. If he had been less
demanding, perhaps his music would be played more often. At
the same time, he was able to tolerate and encourage performers
of lesser calibre if circumstances required those responses; for
example, he achieved success in 1967 even with a part-time
orchestra in Malta, which must have tried his patience to the limit
but no doubt satisfied the diplomatic objectives of the British
Council.

An occasion of quite a different kind was the Investiture of the
Prince of Wales at Caernarfon Castle in July 1969, for which Bliss
had been asked by the Earl Marshall, the previous year, to compose the ceremonial music. For this important event, the Band
of the Royal Welsh Fusiliers and the trumpeters of the Royal
Military School of Music were disposed in various parts of the
Castle and the Master was requested to provide antiphonal

1. G. Roscow, op. cit. p272.

fanfares, interspersed with interludes for full military band. The sound was as splendid as the spectacle, for those who watched and heard it on television. It was a commission which Bliss could fulfil better than anyone else in Britain and also enjoy: 'I *do* like *colour* – or anything involving pageantry or ceremony – yes, I *do*,' he said, with such obvious sincerity that not even the most ardent republican could have quibbled.[1]

While he was busy with the 'Investiture Music' and the Cello Concerto, Bliss was also composing two concert pieces for the piano which he offered to Louis Kentner 'in gratitude and admiration'.[2] To these, he finally added a third piece and gave them the title *Triptych*, borrowed from pictorial art, although their individual titles – 'Meditation', 'Dramatic Recitative' and 'Capriccio' – do not have any obvious visual associations. Kentner gave the first performance at a Queen Elizabeth Hall recital, which members of the Bliss family attended, in March 1971, and later the pieces were broadcast.

The variety of these compositions – a concerto for cello and orchestra, ceremonial music for brass, and a rather intellectual group of piano pieces – all composed, or at least completed, within a period of two years, cannot fail to strike a reader as extraordinary. But we must also remember that AB's composition methods were not like those of a cook producing a meal; nothing was prepared, cooked and served in complete stages, everything he wrote was critically examined, played over again and again on the piano, and often revised several times after its première (for example, *Hymn to Apollo* and *Discourse for Orchestra* which were completely re-written years after they were composed). His works have often been admired for their directness, for the immediacy of their impact; but this was achieved by the expenditure of infinite trouble and pains. He was occasionally criticized for the very achievement we have just admired – versatility; his music, it has been said, lacked an individual style because its aims were too diverse, but, in the words of another professional who conducted his music and knew it very well, 'That won't wash. Even in late works, his voice remained as individual as ever (eg the cello concerto).'[3] Besides, Bliss never worried much about general criticism – '... contemptuous references to my music have been so numerous in the last few years,' he wrote to his brother, Howard, in 1961, 'that they almost fail to stir me.'[4] Indeed, self-criticism played a larger part in the mind of AB than any general disapproval of his music from outside; like some of his near-contemporary British composers (for example, Vaughan Williams) he tended to be over-modest, even self-deprecatory. 'I am aware that many of my musical dreams have never become realities,'[5] he wrote on nearly the last page of his autobiography, and the same sort of comment might have been made by VW.:

1. BBC Commemoration Programme – AB interviewed by M. Oliver – 'Arthur Bliss, a contradictory figure'.
2. S. Craggs, op. cit. p192.   3. Vernon Handley, *The Full Score*, Spring 1996, p5.
4. Letter dated 28.9.61. CUL.   5. Bliss, op. cit. p245.

AB and Trudy with Herbert
Howells and his wife, 1972.

'Self-deprecation as a form of modesty was very much the style of his generation and class ...'[1] But censure, from outside or self-inflicted, was certainly not part of the celebrations surrounding AB on August 1971 for his eightieth birthday, which was greeted by rejoicing in many parts of the world as well as in Britain. In London, the orchestral players who held him in such high regard presented him with a specially recorded disc containing selections from his music; this was at a Promenade Concert in the Albert Hall on the actual birthday, August 2nd, at which he conducted *Music for Strings*. The opening bars of this work appeared in sugar on a cake presented to him the previous week at a party in the Victoria and Albert Museum. And there were, of course, family celebrations as well, at which, no doubt several choice 'Blissisms' (or off-the-cuff chestnuts) were uttered. The best recorded one, however, was his famous exclamation – 'What a lovely thing it is to be 80!'[2]

Two months previously, Bliss received the CH (Companion of Honour) from the Queen and so, mature in years, revered with honours and affectionately admired by his peers, he might reasonably have been expected to retire from his life's work of composition. But retirement, in most of its senses, was not his style; the fact that he was eighty made no difference to his philosophy of life and work: 'I like work. I think it does you good. I'm always working.'[3] That was his style, and a remark of Vaughan Williams about Elgar could equally well be applied in this context

1. Michael Kennedy, 'Voyages of an English Mystic', *Sunday Telegraph Review.* 10.9.95, p8.
2. In a letter to George Dannatt, with kind permission.
3. See p.157, Miss D. Maxwell.

to Bliss: 'I think it is part of Elgar's greatness that he realised so fully that the style is the man.'[1] But in the final count, it was not the compulsion to work which made him go on composing music after his eightieth birthday, it was, as he said, 'the sheer love of it.' Arthur Bliss simply loved writing music. As one of his daughters expressed it, 'His best composition, in his opinion, was "the next one".'[2] And so he continued to supply an eclectic stream of compositions for the next three years, some very short works – for example, an *Ode for Sir William Walton*, for his seventieth birthday; an anthem *Put thou thy trust in the Lord*, for the Silver Wedding Service of the Queen and the Duke of Edinburgh at Westminster Abbey: and a *Wedding Suite* (piano solo) for Enid, AB's half-sister, who married Thomas Frame-Thompson in January 1974. This last work (largely a recreation of a very early work, *Valses Fantastiques*, of 1913) had strong personal associations for AB: Enid was the daughter of Mr F.E. Bliss's third marriage and had been a child-bridesmaid at Arthur and Trudy's wedding at Santa Barbara in 1925. She and her mother continued to live in California after Mr Bliss died but made frequent visits to London, much to AB's pleasure because he found in Enid many of his father's traits and interests.[3] Her late marriage in London therefore gave him particular joy.

There were also two major works during this last period of Bliss's career as a composer: a big orchestral set of variations and a cantata for solo voices, chorus and organ. The second of these, called *Shield of Faith* was a commission from the Windsor Festival Committee who wanted to commemorate in music the five-hundred-year-history of St George's Chapel; thus the poems which Bliss set, chosen for him by Canon Verney, represent an author from each of the five centuries: William Dunbar (16th century), George Herbert (17th) Alexander Pope (18th), Lord Tennyson (19th) and T.S. Eliot (20th). An anthology of texts with such wide disparity of period was no novelty for Bliss (see *Morning Heroes* and *Pastoral*), but from his own programme-note it sounds as if he was especially inspired by two of them: *Love* by Herbert and the extracts from 'Little Gidding', Eliot's fourth of the *Four Quartets*: Bliss was fond of reading poetry aloud – he did enjoy the sound of his voice and often read aloud to his family when the children were young[4] – and the rhythm of the verse in both these examples, Herbert and Eliot, was probably of more importance to him than the precise meaning which, in the case of the Eliot, he confessed to not grasping fully. But the general tone of a work of art – literary or visual – was all that Bliss needed to assimilate in order to reproduce it musically, *provided* it was beautiful in the original.

1. 'Elgar Today', *Musical Times*, June 1957, p302.
2. Mrs K. Sellick, in conversation with the author.
3. Bliss, op. cit. p193.
4. Mrs K. Sellick, with kind permission.

The significance of beauty, in the abstract, in Bliss's life and work would make a good study for a thesis; there are plenty of references to it in the autobiography but it has not figured largely in the profiles which have been written about him; more often, the ugly images of war or the nervous tensions of his film and ballet music have coloured the personality which has emerged. Maybe a revival of *Shield of Faith* would help to redress the balance. The work was dedicated, by 'Gracious Permission', to HM Queen Elizabeth II and first performed in St George's Chapel exactly a month after Sir Arthur died.

The other large work of his last period was *Metamorphic Variations* for full orchestra. The scale of this music, apart from other factors, merits an attentive survey of it. It begins and ends with a plaintive, unaccompanied song on the oboe, a lone voice which might represent the spirit of Bliss himself starting and finishing his journey through life. This is the first of the three 'elements' announced in the first section on which, the composer tells us in

Interior of St George's Chapel, Windsor. Bliss composed *Shield of Faith* for its Quincentenary celebration. (Reproduced by permission of the Dean and Canons of Windsor)

118

his programme-note, the whole work is based. Three themes and variations then? Not exactly. That would be too simple. The word metamorphic in the title was added, he explained because the three 'elements' go through greater changes than would be tolerable if the following sections were merely 'variations'. This warning is amply fulfilled after about ten minutes of listening: 'Assertion', 'Speculation', 'Interjection', 'Contemplation' – all go by with little obvious reference to the basic 'elements', unless one can follow a score. But (and this is an important qualification) each section describes a mood and each mood is different, like a patchwork counterpane; the moods are highlighted, in true Bliss fashion, by superb contrasts of orchestration, rhythm and pace; the interest is held even if the intellect has failed to comprehend where our Maestro is leading us. And then we arrive at a dance – very identifiable – and see from the programme that it is a 'Polonaise', effectively enlivened by what sound like castanets; but event as we relax and enjoy the infectious rhythm we begin to suspect that the cavorting trumpet is leading us astray with some rather unexpected sounds and sure enough, when he reaches a top note all the others stop playing and we are gently ushered into a 'Funeral Procession'.

Bliss himself did caution us against sameness. Variety, he said, is what this work is all about. So we allow the funeral march to pass slowly by (it is the second-longest of the fourteen sections), remembering that he composed a special march for the funeral-day of Sir Winston Churchill in 1965, and we enjoy the next three sections. The third ('Duet') is a wonderful dialogue between solo violin and cello, showing off their respective qualities to perfection. Now we are into the 'Dedication', a rousing fanfare for blazoning brass, and in the programme we are told that these splendidly hearty instruments are proclaiming in musical notation the initials of the dedicatees of this work – G.D. and A.D.

George and Ann Dannatt had long been close friends of Arthur and Trudy Bliss. They met each year at the Cheltenham Festival and there the two men often spent a morning nattering about music (Dannatt had been a professional music critic) or visiting a local art exhibition (he is a noted abstract painter), while their wives went off into the countryside on a nature ramble, an interest which they shared. When the Dannatts were away from their home on the Dorset-Wiltshire border, they occasionally lent it to the Blisses for short visits and it was on one of these, in June 1972, that AB found inspiration for his ninth variation (the 'Funeral Processions') from some of his friend's paintings. He so much appreciated the Dannatts' generosity in lending their house in the country that he decided to affirm their friendship by dedicating the whole work to them jointly. Having done so, he was willing – typically – to invite comment on it. While rehearsing it on one occasion after its completion, he turned to Dannatt and said, 'George! we will go through with the rehearsal and if you don't like it stand up and say so, and we will stop and all go

Arthur and Trudy Bliss on holiday with George and Ann Dannatt. AB dedicated *Metamorphic Variations* to them. (Courtesy of George Dannatt)

home.'[1] This was not intended to be taken seriously!

And so we reach the last and longest section of the work, 'Affirmation', a warm and powerful statement by the whole orchestra to begin with but quickly subsiding into a strangely anguished mood – turbulent in places – as if the composer was undergoing a final struggle to release a daemon within. And at last it is banished, after a great climax, with a shattering blow on the tam-tam (large gong) and with what has been described as a 'chord of disintegration', in which the three motifs of the work are 'exploded', or pulled apart, before returning to the opening oboe melody.[2] The daemon has been expelled at last and the spirit soars away as the oboe ends the work in the way it began.

In some respects, *Metamorphic Variations* reveal more of Arthur Bliss than any single one of his previous works. Several of the titles he gave each section provide a pointer to some aspect of his character: the inclusion of 'Ballet' as the first variation is of obvious significance; 'Assertion', which comes next, is surely a reference to his early works; the two 'Scherzos' relate to his constant bustle and 'dash'; 'Contemplation' and 'Cool Interlude' recall his deep reading and intellectual interests. The musical content of these 'Variations' is not only apt to the mood of each one but also characteristic of the composer's work. As one writer has observed, the music 'exemplifies the development and embodies the essence of Bliss's long creative life.'[3] The work was first performed with the title *Variations for Orchestra* by the LSO, conducted by Vernon Handley at the Fairfield Hall, Croydon, on 21 April 1973. Nearly two years later, in January 1975, there was a recording by the BBC Symphony Orchestra, conducted again by Handley, at which Bliss was present. It was the last performance of one of his major works which he heard before his death, and unfortunately there is no record of his reaction to it on that occa-

1. George Dannatt, with kind permission.
2. George Dannatt, Notes for 'Nimbus' NU 5294, 1991, with permission.
3. A. Burn, 'Bliss's music 1966-75', op. cit. p296.

The score of the start of *Variation VII* ('Contemplation').

sion. But in a recorded interview in the spring of the previous year, he allowed himself the following remarkable reflection:

Curiously enough, you see, I haven't really reached, I'm not old enough to have reached, serenity, in my music. I notice, for instance, in the *Variations*, how violent some of them are.[1]

From a man of his age, the confession is astonishing for it shows that he never lost the dynamo which had driven him in his work for the past fifty years. The 'violence' which he 'notices' in *Metamorphic Variations* was clearly sub-conscious at its creation,

1. Quoted by George Dannatt in Notes for 'Nimbus' recording, op. cit.

121

which raises the question of whether he ever really recovered completely from the experience of the First World War. In describing his personal reasons for composing *Morning Heroes*, he wrote: 'If sublimation, the externalising of an obsession, can be thought of as a cure, then in my case I have proved its efficacy'.[1] But, as one writer has observed:

When we think of the experience of the First World War as one of the corner-stones of Bliss's creativity, the picture changes radically. Was the experience of these years directly responsible for that unmistakable streak of violence which has broken out sporadically in Bliss's music ever since, and which has, in fact, resulted in some of his finest and most convincing utterances? ... He claimed that 'Morning Heroes' effectively consigned this spectre to oblivion. One wonders ...[2]

In a BBC Radio Programme about *Morning Heroes*[3] of more recent date, some extracts from letters written to Bliss by his brother, Kennard, before he was killed in 1916, were read. The overwhelming emotion which these extracts convey is Kennard's bitter anger at the appalling waste of life he witnessed during the early stages of the Somme battle. In that battle his brother Arthur, now a Captain, who had recently been 'Mentioned in Despatches', had been wounded and was now recovering in England. In almost his last letter from the Front, dated July 31st 1916, Kennard wrote: '(Apologies for so serious a letter at this gay event, but levity is not fitting in war!) Dear A, I very much doubt if this letter will reach you on your birthday, but it may make a good attempt...', and ends, 'And so farewell, and fervent wishes that next year's August 2nd will find the wound (in your brain) healed, never to re-open'.[4]

Bliss dearly loved his brother and greatly respected his intellect. He dedicated *Morning Heroes* 'To the memory of my brother FRANCIS KENNARD BLISS and other comrades killed in battle.' Its main quality is compassion; it glorifies heroes, not war. This fact has been emphasized by many of AB's friends and admirers, not least by his wife who followed its creation with close involvement as she did all his compositions. It was her calming influence which gave AB the rest and composure he needed, yet she was able to discuss his work with him on a level commensurate with its riches; she had the insight to know when to criticize and when to encourage, and she made him homes which he loved – East Heath Lodge, Pen Pits, 8 The Lane. In nearly all his frequent travels abroad, especially to America, she was his willing companion and there were occasions when she even persuaded him to forsake the speed of air-travel in favour of a ship; '... so here was another charming

1. Bliss, op. cit. p96.
2. C. Palmer, 'Novello Short Biography', 1976.
3. The 'Making of Morning Heroes', BBC Radio 3, 8 Nov 1985.
4. Bliss, op. cit. p43.
5. Bliss, op. cit. (Ch. xxvi by Trudy Bliss).

'His carefully written speeches ...' AB presenting prizes at the Royal Military School of Music, Kneller Hall, in 1961, flanked by Lt Col D. McBain (left) and Bandmaster T.L. Sharpe (right).

point of repose', she wrote afterwards, 'a whole week at sea.'[5] They were generous hosts, at home or abroad, and she was an ideal hostess, producing marvellous meals – often from American recipes – while he regaled the guests with anecdotes, often accompanied by hilarious mime. The guests might include people like the Boults, the Mayers, Walton, Ralph Richardson, and Moura Lympany, and talk was all about the current musical or theatrical news. In earlier times, his daughters remember family charades, and their father reading to them at bed time. If it were Sherlock Holmes stories it seemed to them that '... he always managed to almost reach the climax before saying, 'That's all for to-night, we'll finish it to-morrow'.[1] It was a happy household, due to the love of both parents.

What AB called 'real' happiness was uppermost in his philosophy of life. To him, this kind of happiness was not of the hedonistic, self-indulgent sort; he defined it, rather, as 'some kind of heaven ... *within* ourselves'.[2] and that implied a search for the

1. Mrs B. Gatehouse, with kind permission.
2. Bliss, op. pit. p277.

A picture of happiness – Sir Arthur in January 1975, two months before his death.
(Photo by Tony McGrath, *Observer*)

truth within our own characters. This philosophy he expounded in a speech to the young undergraduates of Westminster Choir College, Princeton, New Jersey, in June 1968, an address he had been invited to make as a result of the College Choir's performance of *The Beatitudes* in New York the previous year. It was an occasion rather like a school Speech Day in this country, when a guest speaker can leave his audience snoring; but AB's talk (reproduced *verbatim* in Lady Bliss's Coda to his autobiography, Chapter xxvi) is a clever mixture of good sense, good history and good advice, unpretentious and modest. As he was addressing a musical audience he ended by explaining how music fitted into his theme:

music is an art that reaches beyond the world, as well as being one of the great sources of happiness. Endless draughts of peace and healing can be drawn from its mysterious depths.[1]

In short, 'some kind of heaven within ourselves', which might aptly serve as an epitaph for Arthur Bliss.

He died on 27 March 1975, aged eighty-three, having had an operation for cancer the previous year. During that year's remission, he was – typically – more interested in completing some unfinished work than in the cause of his illness: 'He preferred to

1. Bliss, op. cit. p278.

think that the doctors knew their job, being professionals, and if they failed ... that was it.'[1] The death of a public figure of such stature was naturally followed, two months later, by a memorial service in Westminster Abbey, at which Sir David Willcocks gave the Address, and by many obituaries and tributes from all parts of the world. But what Bliss himself would surely most of all hope for is a renewal of interest in his music and that, thanks to the formation of the Bliss Trust in 1986, is now well under way; the Trust has sponsored a number of CD recordings of his works, and, besides further recordings, has plans to establish a scholarship for promising musicians from Britain to continue their studies in the USA. When he was reflecting on the death of his predecessor, Sir Arnold Bax, as Master of the Queen's Musick, Sir Arthur wrote:

During my seventy-five years I have seen many reputations rise and sink ... Musical reputations seem to move around like the slats on a watermill, first ascending to a peak of admiration, then descending to a depth of neglect, before once more climbing the ascent towards renewed appreciation.[2]

When we recall the determination of his early years, the skill of his maturity, and the perseverance of his old age, we can appreciate the size and quality of his gift to posterity – over one hundred and thirty works. Their 'ascent towards renewed appreciation' is now happening.

1. Mrs K. Sellick, with kind permission.
2. Bliss, op. cit. p192.

Select Bibliography

Reference

The following books of reference on Bliss and his music are now available in most music libraries:

Craggs, S.R., *Arthur Bliss: a Bio-Bibliography*, (Greenwood Press, 1988)

Craggs, S.R., *Arthur Bliss – a Source Book*, (Scolar Press, 1996)

Foreman, L., *Arthur Bliss: Catalogue of the Complete Works*, with Introduction by George Dannatt (Novello, 1980)
(A Supplement to the above, compiled by G. Easterbrook and Lady Bliss was published in 1982.)

Roscow, G. (ed), *Bliss on Music – Selected Writings of Arthur Bliss, 1920–1975*, (OUP 1991)

Burn, A. (ed), *Bliss Centenary Brochure*, (The Bliss Trust, 1988)

Novello & Co Ltd, *Arthur Bliss* (Profile and Work List) (Novello, 1995)

Biographical

Palmer, C., *Bliss*, (Novello Short Biographies Series, 1995)

Bliss, A., *As I Remember* (autobiography), (Faber & Faber, 1970; new ed. Thames Publishing, 1989)

The *Dictionary of National Biography* ('DNB') has an article on Bliss by George Dannatt and, as always, Grove's 'Dictionary of Music and Musicians' (*The New Grove Dictionary of Music* 1980) is enlightening on the man and his music.

General

Books on British music and musicians during the fifty-five years (1920–1975) of Bliss's active musical life are not so plentiful as one might expect but abundant enough to require a ruthless selection here:

'The Cambridge Cultural History of Britain' (Vols 8 and 9) (C.U.P./Folio Society, 1995)

Banfield, S., *Sensibility and English Song: critical studies of the early twentieth century*, Vol 2, (CUP 1985)

Beaumont, C., *The Sadler's Wells Ballet*, (London, 1946)

Briggs, A., *The History of Broadcasting in the UK* (Vol IV) (BBC 1979)

Fussell, P., *The Great War and Modern Memory*, (OUP 1975)

Howes, F., *The English Musical Renaissance,* (London, 1966)

Lambert, C., *Music Ho! A Study of Music in Decline,* (London, 1934, reprinted 1966)

Moore, J.N., *Edward Elgar – a Creative Life,* (OUP 1984)

Salzman, E., *Twentieth-Century Music: an Introduction* (2nd Ed), (Prentice-Hall, Inc. 1974)

Trend, M., *The Music Makers: Heirs and Rebels of the English Musical Renaissance from Elgar to Britten,* (London, 1985)

Wood, H.J., *My Life of Music,* (Gollancz, 1938)

Scores and Recordings

Scores

A large proportion (although not all) of Bliss's music was published by Novello, and these scores are still available. Potential purchasers should ask their suppliers to contact the following address, quoting 'Special Order':
Novello & Co. Ltd. (Distribution), Newmarket Road, Bury St. Edmunds, Suffolk IP33 3YB
(Tel: 01284 702600; Fax: 01284 703401)

Recordings
(Compact Discs, and Cassettes where indicated)

A Colour Symphony; Adam Zero (complete ballet)
    English Northern Philharmonia/ David Lloyd-Jones
    Naxos 8.553460

A Colour Symphony; Metamorphic variations
    BBC Welsh SO/Barry Wordsworth
    Nimbus NI 5294
    (also cassette: NC 5294)

A Colour Symphony, Introduction and Allegro, Men of Two Worlds, Baraza, Things to Come (suite and excerpts)
    LSO/Composer (and others)
    Dutton Laboratories CDLXT 2501

Checkmate – ballet
    English Northern Philharmonia/ David Lloyd-Jones
    Hyperion CDA 66436

Things to Come – suite; *Welcome the Queen*
    LSO/Composer
    Belart 450 143-2
    (also cassette, 450 143-4)

Morning Heroes
    John Westbrook/LPChoir/LPO/ Sir Charles Groves
    EMI CDM 7 63906 2

Music for Strings; Pastoral
    Northern Sinfonia/Richard Hickox
    Chandos CHAN 8886
    (also cassette: ABTD 1497)

Piano Concerto; March of Homage
    Philip Fowke/RLPO/David Atherton
    Unicorn UKCD 2029
    (also cassette, UKC 2029)

'Cello Concerto, etc.
    Raphael Wallfisch/Ulster Orch/ Vernon Handley
    Chandos CHAN 8818
    (also cassette, ABTD 1443)

Clarinet Quintet
    Janet Hilton/Lindsay String Quartet
    Chandos CHAN 8683
    (also cassette, ABTD 1078)

Viola Sonata; also *Masks, Triptych, Two Interludes, Toccata* (piano)
    Emanuel Vardi/Kathron Sturrock
    Chandos CHAN 8770
    (also cassette, ABTD 1408)

String Quartets Nos. 1 & 2
    Delmé Quartet
    Hyperion CDA 66178

Piano Sonata, and other pieces
    Philip Fowke
    Chandos CHAN 8979
    (also cassette: ABTD 1567)

Kenilworth Suite
    Black Dyke Mills Band/Peter Parkes
    Chandos CHAN 4505
    (also cassette, BBTD 4506)

Rout, Rhapsody, Conversation, Women of Yueh, Madame Noy; also *Oboe Quintet*
    Elizabeth Gale/Anthony Rolfe Johnson/Nash Ensemble/ Lionel Friend
    Hyperion CDA66 137

The following recording is not currently available but is to be found in second-hand record shops:
    'Campoli Classics III'
    (*Violin Concerto, Theme and Cadenza for Violin and Orchestra*)
    Alfredo Campoli/LPO/Composer
    Burah 3PD 10

Index

*Illustrations are indicated in **bold** type*

130

		DATE DUE	